HUMAN RELATIONSHIPS

Philosophical Introductions

Series editors: Anthony Ellis and Gordon Graham

HUMAN RELATIONSHIPS

A PHILOSOPHICAL INTRODUCTION

Paul Gilbert

BLACKWELL
Oxford UK & Cambridge USA

First published 1991

Basil Blackwell Ltd
108 Cowley Road, Oxford, OX4 1JF, UK

Basil Blackwell, Inc.
3 Cambridge Center
Cambridge, Massachusetts 02142, USA

Library of Congress Cataloging in Publication Data
Gilbert, Paul (Paul H.)
Human relationships a philosophical introduction/Paul Gilbert.
    p.   cm. — (Philosophical introductions)
Includes bibliographical references and index.
ISBN 0–631–17157–6 (alk. paper): — ISBN 0–631–17158–4 (pbk.):
1. Love—Philosophy. 2. Friendship—Philosophy. 3. Social sciences—
    Philosophy.   I. Title.   II. Series.
    BD436.G55   1991
    177'.6—dc20   91–12475
                                                         CIP

British Library Cataloguing in Publication Data
A CIP catalogue record for this book is available from the British Library.

Typeset in 10 on 12 pt Garamond
by Graphicraft Typesetters Ltd., Hong Kong
Printed in Great Britain by T.J. Press Ltd., Padstow, Cornwall.

This book is printed on acid-free paper.

Contents

Acknowledgements

I am grateful to numerous colleagues and students, at Hull and elsewhere, for useful suggestions and criticisms; and, in particular, to Gordon Graham, the series editor, for helpful advice and encouragement, to Michael Smithurst and David Walker for reading individual chapters, and, most of all, to Kathleen Lennon for scrutinizing and improving the whole book in draft.

In chapter 4 I have re-used some material from my paper, 'Friendship and the Will', in *Philosophy*, vol. 61 (1986): my thanks to the editor and publishers.

My acknowledgements are due to the following for permission to quote from the copyright works indicated: the extract from Edward Albee's *Who's Afraid of Virginia Woolf?* is reprinted with permission of Edward Albee, Jonathan Cape and Atheneum Publishers (copyright © 1962, renewed 1990 by Edward Albee); the extracts from the works of Elizabeth Bowen are reprinted with permission of the Estate of Elizabeth Bowen and Jonathan Cape, and of Alfred A. Knopf Inc. for 'The Death of the Heart' and 'The Heat of the Day' from *The Collected Stories of Elizabeth Bowen* (copyright © 1981 by Curtis Brown Ltd) and of Curtis Brown Ltd, London, for *The Hotel*.

Last, but not least, I wish to thank Margaret Snowden and Audrey Solly for turning my tapes into a typescript.

Paul Gilbert
Department of Philosophy
University of Hull

For Daphne

1

Society, Friendship and Love

1.1 Philosophy and Social Life

I am monarch of all I survey;
My right there is none to dispute;
From the centre all round to the sea
I am Lord of the fowl and the brute.
O Solitude! Where are the charms
That sages have seen in thy face?
Better dwell in the midst of alarms
Than reign in this horrible place ...

Society, Friendship, and Love
Divinely bestowed upon man,
O had I the wings of a dove
How soon would I taste you again!
My sorrows I then might assuage
In the ways of religion and truth,
Might learn from the wisdom of age,
And be cheer'd by the sallies of youth.

Thus laments the unhappy original of Daniel Defoe's Robinson Crusoe, in William Cowper's poem 'The Solitude of Alexander Selkirk'. But we do not need to find ourselves on a desert island to reflect upon the importance of social relations in our lives. What can account for the powerful hold that these relationships have over us? What exactly do they consist in, and why do we enter into them?

Such reflections can take many forms. Every society has myths about its own origins which shape the individual's attitude to his or her place in it. Our own society is no exception. Consider, for example, the novelist and 'progressive' thinker, H. G. Wells.

> Probably the earliest human societies, in the opening stages of the true human story, were small family groups. Just as the flocks and herds of the earlier mammals arose out of families which remained together and multiplied, so probably did the earlier tribes. But before this could happen, a certain restraint upon the primitive egotisms of the individuals had to be established. The fear of the father and respect for the mother had to be extended into adult life, and the natural jealousy of the old man of the group for the younger males as they grew up had to be mitigated. The mother, on the other hand, was the natural adviser and protector of the young. Human social life grew up out of the reaction between the crude instinct of the young to go off and pair by themselves as they grew up, on the one hand, and the dangers and disadvantages of the isolation on the other. (Wells, p. 42)

And why might one believe this? As *history* it is pure speculation. No evidence is offered for it, and indeed it is hard to imagine what evidence could be collected. Sheep, it seems, have acquired a flocking instinct which their predecessors lacked. But gregariousness has been bred into them through domestication by man. It is difficult to see how a similar process could occur spontaneously in humans. And indeed no such process leading to a *change* in instinctual human behaviour is seriously being suggested by Wells. For we are meant to recognize 'the primitive egotisms' of the individual, 'the natural jealousy of the old' and 'the crude instinct of the young to go off and pair' in the *present* behaviour of people. We are invited to extrapolate these tendencies from their occurrence *within* human society to an imagined past time preceding it, and to wonder how society could grow on such unpromising soil. But we would only be inclined to do that, of course, if we felt that these tendencies were somehow *fundamental* to human nature itself – and for that Wells again offers us no evidence. His assumptions about human nature are, we might say, purely mythic ones.

Contrast Wells's story with that of the anarchist thinker, Prince Peter Kropotkin.

> Far from being a primitive form of organisation, the family is a very late product of human evolution. As far us we can go back in the palaeo-ethnology of mankind, we find men living in societies – in tribes similar to those of the higher mammals, and an extremely slow and long evolution was required to bring these societies to the gentile, or clan organisation, which, in its turn, had to undergo another, also very long evolution,

before the first germs of family, polygamous or monogamous, could appear. Societies, bands, or tribes – not families – were thus the primitive form of organisation of mankind and its earliest ancestors. That is what ethnology has come to after its painstaking researches. And in so doing it simply came to what might have been foreseen by the zoologist ... The first human societies simply were a further development of those societies which constitute the very essence of life of the higher animals. (Kropotkin, p. 76)

As history this is also speculation. As natural history it is confused about the scope of evolutionary explanation. As an empirical description of present-day societies, however, it is more credible than Wells's. It simply observes that everywhere we look people live in societies, and in only some of them are there what we would recognize as family units. And in only some, we might add, jealousy on the part of the old or pairing off on the part of the young. Yet Kropotkin too is driven by a picture – as mythic in its hold on him as Wells's – a picture of the natural sociability of humankind.

These contrasting pictures of human nature – egotistical versus sociable; prudential versus spontaneous; disruptive versus supportive – are presented not just as *optional* ways of looking at people, as a novelist might depict the characters now as one type, now as another. They are presented as the *truth* about them. And because in our society claims to truth must show their credentials, Wells and Kropotkin trick out their pictures with the trappings of history or of science. They purport to be based on empirical observation because that seems to be the best guarantee of truth. But when we ask whether these observations strongly confirm them, we find that they do not: the pictures are, at best, compatible with what has been observed.

The pictures recommend themselves to their authors – and are intended to recommend themselves to us – a priori, that is to say, independently of further empirical investigation. They purport to show how human beings *must* be, given what we do want to say about them and their social relationships. But in that case what kind of truths could they purvey?

One reaction will be to deny that there are truths of this kind to be had here, and to claim that the empirical facts exhaust the truths there are. Then different pictures of human nature and society will only seem to conflict; as a gloomy and a pessimistic novel may seem to do, though neither presents itself as showing us how things *are*, rather than how we can *choose* to view them. And this is one way in which what are thought of as *metaphysical* statements – very general a priori statements about how the world must be – are sometimes treated, as akin to literature in shaping attitudes rather than to science in stating truths.

But this surely overlooks two crucial points which distinguish metaphysical from literary descriptions of human nature and society. First, the metaphysical description purports to tell us how people must be if our ordinary empirical descriptions of them are to find a foothold. Unless people are naturally sociable, some might say, our talk of disinterested friendship and co-operation would surely be an illusion. Unless they were primitively egotistical, others might say, our explanations of their social acts in terms of their individual motives would not be cogent. We may be prepared to give up some of our empirical descriptions, but for the most part we cannot. So we are committed to finding some general account of the way people are that makes sense of them. It is the philosopher's task to adjudicate between competing pictures; for, assuming that the empirical descriptions we want to hold on to are not radically incoherent, not all of them should be acceptable. The novelist, by contrast, proposes no such fundamental account of human nature: we can accept or reject her view of it without further consequences for our everyday ways of describing each other's thoughts and actions.

The second difference is that the metaphysical description purports to tell us what our attitudes to people ought to be, how we ought to behave in society, for whether people are naturally sociable or egotistical, say, makes a difference as to how we are to respond to them. It is not enough to declare that we can simply *choose* what attitude we should adopt: which we adopt will determine the ideals and aspirations that we have. For the anarchist, Kropotkin, for example, the ideal society is one without restrictions and restraints where people live in harmony and tranquillity. But it would be pointless to have such an ideal if it rested on a view of human nature which there was no reason to accept. Tolerance of widely divergent ideals may be the hallmark of a liberal society, and 'any diminution in this variety would impoverish the human scene' (Strawson, p. 29). Yet this is not to say that those ideals should not be rationally debated. We try to find reasons for what we think to be worthwhile. And in doing so we are seeking ends that people should pursue.

The influential English philosopher G. E. Moore suggested that *personal affection* was one of two such ultimate ends (Moore, pp. 188–9). In recommending it to us – human beings as we are – he presupposes a view of how we are, of what sort of motives we can have. And if we can be persuaded of the supreme desirability of this end we confirm the truth of his presupposition about us.

There is no sharp distinction, then, between how we are and how we ought to be. Statements about the former imply statements about the latter, since they demand certain attitudes of us as the right ones to take. And statements about the latter imply ones about the former, since accepting statements about what we ought to be, adopting certain attitudes, shows how we are, what we are capable of. It seems evident, by contrast, that the novelist's presentation of human life, while it can get us to see people in a new light, does not recommend such attitudes to us as mandatory, as required or ruled out by the way people are. The novelist seeks, imaginatively, to extend our options; the philosopher, rationally, to restrict them.

None of this is to deny that novelists themselves hold metaphysical theories and express them in their novels. It is just that novels – being works of fiction – do not present these metaphysical theories as facts about the world. On the other hand, works of biology, psychology, sociology or history do aim to present facts about the world, facts whose support comes from empirical observation. Yet these too, as we have seen from the admittedly inexpert examples of H. G. Wells and Kropotkin, commonly make metaphysical assumptions. They go beyond their evidence to paint a more general picture which has repercussions for the terms in which we are to think of people, and the attitudes we are to take up towards them. And when theories in other subjects make such assumptions it is a philosophical task to detect and assess them.

Yet what sort of truth can the philosopher claim for his or her statements? It is certainly not truth based on empirical observation; or rather, not based on observations beyond those that all of us have made in the course of learning how to describe the world and the doings of people in it. As a result the truths philosophers seek do not derive from specialized discoveries: they consist in gaining a clearer view of the commonplace assumptions we make in our everyday thinking about the world, and in assessing the coherence and inescapability of this way of thinking. That is why everyone who engages in such thinking – and that means all of us – is in an equally good position to participate in philosophical discussion. The kind of truth such discussions aim at is the kind that we ascribe on the basis of agreement – if we can reach it – on what our thinking shall be.

We shall need then, to compare the kind of thinking about the world and ourselves that we should have to adopt if we were to accept the metaphysical assumptions sometimes made by psychologists or sociologists with the thinking we already ordinarily engage in. Would it involve drastic changes and would these changes be supportable? Conversely, if the empirical claims that psychologists or sociologists make are true, are the assumptions that lie behind our ordinary thinking threatened, or can we still hold on to them? One thing at least is clear, we must participate in some of these ordinary ways of thinking if we are to continue to live in human society at all. We should be cautious, to say the least, before adopting views that would make that impossible, since it is hard to see how the possibility of social life could depend upon an illusion.

The eighteenth-century philosopher David Hume notoriously thought that reason drove us to reject the views on which ordinary life depended, so that,

> since reason is incapable of dispelling these clouds, Nature herself suffices to that purpose, and cures me of this philosophical melancholy and delirium ... I dine, I play a game of backgammon, I converse and am merry with my friends; and when after three or four hours' amusement, I would return to these speculations, they appear, so cold, and strained, and ridiculous, that I cannot find in my heart to enter into them any further. (Hume, (T), I. iv. 7)

But 'reason' is not, as Hume seems to have supposed, a faculty to be principally employed when 'I am tired with amusement and company, and have indulged a *reverie* in my chamber, or in a solitary walk by a riverside' (ibid.). It is, in fact, principally employed *in company*, in discussion with others who can teach us, if not religion, as Alexander Selkirk muses, then certainly *truth*. For something can count as a reason only if it can command social acceptance as indicative of the truth.

In offering an account of social relationships, therefore, we seek the reasonable agreement of people who are already participants within them. And so we need to ask whether the account makes sense of the way we, as participants, must think. Our interest, then, is not purely academic: it is an interest we have in becoming clearer about what we are doing, and cannot but do, in the course of our social lives. Just as Alexander Selkirk reflects upon the need for society from a keen but inexplicable sense of its absence, so our own reflections must be motivated by an apprehension of the mysterious force it exerts upon us. The questions we ask about it can only be addressed by an account that offers to leave us, as participants, less troubled, more certain about our social lives.

1.2   *Problems: Personal and Philosophical*

Loneliness was Alexander Selkirk's only personal problem. For the rest of us social life generates a host of problems concerning our relationships with others. No one should think that the philosopher – by contrast, perhaps, with the clinical psychologist or the counsellor – can solve them. But our ways of thinking about relationships may create obstacles in the way of solutions, at the social as well as at the personal level, which philosophical clarification and criticism can remove.

Take love. That can lead to the deepest pain as well as to the intensest pleasure. 'What is happening to me? What am I doing?' I ask, unsure whether I am helpless or in control; whether it is love I feel, or *just* desire; whether I want to share, or to possess; whether she is what I imagine her to be or whether I am deluded by infatuation. Each of us must find out the answers to such questions for ourselves as best we can. But these particular and personal problems are evidently related to more general and philosophical ones: Is love voluntary of involuntary? Is it *just* a biological drive or something more? Does it spring from a desire for power or for self-sacrifice? Is it possible to know another well, and if so, how? If you think, for example, that love is just sexual desire, then you will be likely to suppose your own state is involuntary and irrational. You may suppose it matters not what your loved one is really like, since your view of them will simply reflect your desire anyway. Love comes, and goes: no rational assessment of its value is possible. None can figure, then, in any effective deliberations as to what to do. It is evident that with such beliefs one would approach a practical problem about the place of love in one's life very differently from someone who did not share them.

It is these sorts of questions about love which we shall begin by asking, before moving to questions about our relationships more generally. In chapter 2 we examine whether love is only a species of sexual desire, and in particular of desire thought of as simply a biological drive. It is not so easy to incorporate this kind of view into a coherent outlook on life as may be supposed from the description of its practical application in the preceding paragraph. But, someone might say, isn't the view forced on us by science anyway? Whatever the *facts* of science, as we shall see, science is not equipped to provide us with a comprehensive way of looking at our own practical problems.

In chapter 3 we look at accounts of love in terms of the individual motives of lovers. Is love necessarily egotistical? Is it inescapably one-sided? In particular, is the feminist criticism that love inevitably favours men well founded? We see here how questions about how to live our own particular lives connect with questions as to how social life should be led in general, what sorts of relationship are worthwhile and what are not.

The *value* of love is investigated in chapter 4. What do we take ourselves to be aiming at when we are in love? A potent source of personal problems is the *tension* that can be felt between the aims of love and of sexuality. Can we think of love in a way that reconciles them? Or, more generally, conflict is felt between what each wants for themselves from love, and the disinterestedness that love seems to demand. What can constitute a satisfying relationship here?

The question is a large one: we can only go some way towards answering it. But one thing we need for a satisfying relationship, whether it be of love, sexual or familial, or of friendship, is to come to know another well. There are always practical difficulties here. In chapter 5 we distinguish them from the difficulties of principle that some philosophers have erected, but which, as we shall see, are only reflections of neurotic doubt.

Personal relationships demand a measure of privacy: feelings are shared that are not shared with all. But sharing and reciprocity are characteristic of very many social relationships. In chapter 6 we investigate how widely such relationships do and should extend. They can seem oppressive and constricting, limiting the freedom of the individual to act as he or she wishes. Are such criticisms justified in general? Should social practices be organized only to advance the interests of the individuals engaged in them, or can the interests of the social group rationally be given precedence?

The nature of society itself is the subject of chapter 7. Here the contrast between views of human nature as invincibly egotistical or as inherently sociable reappears in a political guise. These views influence our answers to questions like: How should society be run? What should be the role of the state in regulating social life? When can it justifiably be resisted? But these are, fundamentally, questions about what we value, about what sort of social life we consider it worthwhile to have. And the final chapter examines the prospects for, and possible constraints upon, this kind of social improvement.

We end then, as we began, with myths: not myths of the creation of society, which reflect our underlying assumptions about its workings, miscast as history, but myths about its perfect state. And here the myth-maker is on more solid ground, for these myths reflect our aspirations, and cannot be mistaken for the products of empirical discovery. They are evidently open to discussion and disagreement, but, like the hoped-for solutions to all our problems, to practical implementation too.

2

Love and Sex

2.1   *The Pleasures of Love*

In Tolstoy's *Kreutzer Sonata* one of the characters, Pozdnyshev, raises a question that disconcerts his travelling companions.

> 'How is one to understand what is meant by "true love"?' said the gentleman with the glittering eyes timidly and with an awkward smile.
>
> 'Everyone knows what love is' replied the lady, evidently wishing to break off her conversation with him.
>
> 'But I don't', said the man, 'You must define what you understand'.'
>
> 'Why it's very simple', she said, but stopped to consider. 'Love? Love is an exclusive preference for one above everybody else', said the lady.
>
> 'Preference for how long? A month, two days or half an hour', said the grey-haired man, and began to laugh.
>
> 'Excuse me, we are evidently not speaking of the same thing.' 'Oh yes! Exactly the same.' (Tolstoy, (K), p. 99).

They *are* talking about the same thing, or, at least, of what goes under the same name, 'true love', as distinct from the casual affairs the English priggishly call 'amours'. But Pozdnyshev casts doubt on the lady's conception of love which sees a difference of *kind* here. Later he appeals in support to his own experience of married love: 'Amorousness', he says, 'was exhausted by the satisfaction of sensuality and we were left confronting one another in our true relation, that is as two egotists quite alien to each other who wished to get as much pleasure as possible from each other' (ibid., p. 144). There is no such thing as love, he suggests, over and above a species of sexual desire. 'True love' and casual affairs explicitly undertaken for pleasure are the same kind of thing, though the duration, complexity and, in consequence, the problems of the former are no doubt greater.

Pozdnyshev, and it seems to be Tolstoy talking here, arrives at this view from the best of motives: he wants to get clear what love is, and to escape the mystifications of a conventional conception. He has had a particularly pressing and personal reason for doing so that arises from his problems with a relationship. Misconceptions as to their character can adversely affect relationships and thus our lives, as misconceptions about the character of language, say, cannot. Our conceptions shape our attitudes to, and expectations of, our relationships, so that what they are, what in practice they amount to, is not independent of our conceptions of them. Yet our relationships are not shaped solely by our conceptions, which can therefore mislead us as to their potentialities and limitations. We need to keep in mind this *practical* motive, since it partly determines the kind of account of our relationships we seek. It needs to be *usable*. But it must also be soundly based, as a convenient myth is not; for we want to know why a conception that works is workable, and that limits the kinds of factor we can appeal to in arriving at an account. Blood brothers in some African societies may conceive of their relationship as a mystical unity created by the blood exchange. That will not strike us as explaining why they are bound to each other by such strong ties. It is Tolstoy's attempt to meet the requirement that his account of love be soundly based that leads to its being so austere. We *know* that sexual desire is operative in love, while other factors seem less certain. We can be confident of that partly, it seems, because sexual desire has all the status that biology, rather than religion say, confers on it. The pattern exemplified here is a familiar one: some 'reliable' body of knowledge is chosen and an account of our relationships, our lives, our natures, is offered solely in terms of it. What eludes such capture is to be eliminated from rational thought.

We all recognize sexual love, the sort that catches our interest when we hear that unrelated adults or adolescents are in love. Evidently their love involves sexual desire. But what is the relation between such love and the sexual desire involved in it? Tolstoy's suggestion is radical: it is that love is simply one sort of sexual desire. This inverts our pre-reflective picture of sexual love as a kind of *love*, in which sex is one ingredient among others. On Tolstoy's account the phenomena of love are all explicable in terms of sexual desire. Our loving acts are done from sexual desire. Our reasons for loving someone are founded in desire. Since the consequences and antecedents of love are, in this picture, just the consequences and antecedents of sexual desire, there seems no reason not to identify sexual love as a certain sort of sexual desire.

What Tolstoy offers us in the *Kreutzer Sonata* is a *reduction* of love to sexual desire. Reductionism *reduces* the apparent contents of the universe. Love *appears* to be something over and above sexual desire, involving deeper attachment and unselfish concern. The reductionist denies that it really is any more than this. Reductionism is thus a less radical position than *eliminativism*, the view which denies the existence of love altogether, on the grounds that if it existed it would *have* to be other than mere sexual desire, and all that exists in this area is sexual desire. But eliminativism is unattractive except as a rhetorical device. We do talk about love without evident arbitrariness or incoherence, and this is something the eliminativist will find it hard to explain. What the reductionist aims to do is to account for our being able to talk or think about love, even though on his view we go wrong in reflectively thinking that we are talking about something over and above sexual desire. In analogous cases this aim is easily accomplished. We talk, for example, of will-o'-the-wisp, which the reductionist identifies with glowing marsh gas. We wrongly think of it as an elusive sprite, owing to our pre-scientific speculations about the phenomenon. Yet the error does not prevent us from being able correctly to discriminate a real phenomenon. Similarly, reductionism about love views our pre-reflective thinking as based on errors that arise from not looking at sexual love with a clear enough gaze, unbiased by religion or popular romance.

Yet what evidence do we really have that compels us to view sexual love as only a species of sexual desire? Tolstoy's character Pozdnyshev draws on his own unhappy experiences of sexual relationships to support the view. However, taking cases where what *seemed* to be love turned out to be only sexual desire cannot show that there is never any other thing. Indeed, the effectiveness of taking such cases to disabuse us of romantic illusions depends on our having a clear conception of love, by reference to which these cases fall short.

The reductionist can allow this – though Tolstoy does not seem to do so. The reductionist can allow that what distinguishes love from casual sexual relationships is not simply that those we call 'love' last longer. He must however insist that what does distinguish love – the closeness of the bond, concern for the other, or whatever – is itself explicable as a manifestation of desire. It is evident that to establish this much more is required than observations of the dominance of sexuality in love relationships. What is needed is some theoretical framework within which what *appear* to be non-sexual factors can be construed as sexual ones. In particular we need an account of what sort of desire sexual desire may be. Such a framework of theory should be answerable to observations of social behaviour, but what recommends it may be general assumptions about ourselves and the world that are subject to philosophical clarification and scrutiny.

2.2   *The Love of Pleasure*

Let us first consider one plausible, but thoroughly confused, old theory, which might lead us to the Tolstoyan conclusion. Hedonism is the view that all our actions are done for pleasure. All desires, urges the hedonist, are desires for pleasure. When we engage in acts of love we therefore act from a desire for pleasure. In the case of sexual love what sort of pleasure could that be but sexual pleasure? So all acts of love are explicable as done from sexual desire. What obscures this from us is a moralistic revulsion at the principle of hedonism. Under the influence of religion and custom we like to think of our acts as more high-minded than the hedonist seems to allow. But this prevents us from making a rational calculation of what acts maximize pleasure. Acts of love are a tactic for obtaining sexual pleasure, but quite possibly a tactic of very limited efficiency.

Tolstoy himself was not of course a hedonist in general. Yet his attitude to *sexual* relations was clearly one in which he could see no ordinary alternative to a hedonist explanation. For him, then, leaving reproductive aims aside, the choice is between sesual pleasure and celibacy which permits the pursuit of higher goals.

A good example of the full-blown hedonist position is that of the eighteenth-century French Enlightenment philosopher, the Marquis de Sade. In his novel *Justine* we find a sentiment as strikingly anti-sentimental as Pozdnyshev's.

> When I meet a beautiful woman and fall in love with her, I haven't any different aim from the man who sees and desires her without any sort of love. We both wish to go to bed with her; he only wants her body, whereas I, through a false and dangerous metaphysic, blind myself on my real motive which is exactly the same as my rival's, and persuade myself that I merely want her heart. (quoted Gorer, p. 152)

De Sade equates sexual desire with the drive for the physical pleasures of sexual intercourse. Love is thus a self-deceiving and ineffectual form of this desire. Not only is love denied the superior value that it seemed to have through being equated with a sort of sexual desire; it is actually viewed as inferior in value to other — more honest and efficient — kinds of sexuality.

This message is nowadays a familiar, if slightly modish one. There are no doubt better arguments for it than the present one. But some of the same assumptions often arise. While the *general* principle of hedonism may be discarded, versions of it exercise an attraction when applied to activities, like sex, which we want to engage in with no further end in view. Controversy over whether acts of love out-perform casual sex acts in maximizing satisfaction often seems to presuppose the hedonist model. A judgement on the value of love and its proper place in social life thus awaits an investigation of comparative pleasures as solemn for its practitioners as it is comic to detached observers.

The general principle of hedonism – that the ultimate end of action is a desire for pleasure – was a commonplace of nineteenth-century utilitarian thought. Such a principle is thought necessary to explain how one can act to *maximize* satisfaction, discarding, for example, as contemporary 'equity theory' has it (see chapter 3.2, pp. 37–8), those relationships which do not pay off in achieving an overall balance of benefits against costs. Pleasure is the common unit of currency in such calculations and exchanges. Yet this conception of pleasure as the ultimate end of all desire is a confused one. It is evident that to do what one wants gives one pleasure while to have what one wants to be without, for example pain, is unpleasant. But the pleasure of getting what I want presupposes and thus cannot explain desire. It is not a separate feeling of a kind that I would desire to have. Of course there are such feelings: pleasurable sensations that I desire to have, like those of sexual intercourse. However, it seems quite implausible to suppose that all my desires are directed towards obtaining such sensations. I may want to finish a book because I enjoy it, but my enjoyment does not consist in my having pleasurable sensations while reading: rather it consists precisely in my finding myself *wanting* to read on.

Many pleasures, it must be conceded, and the pleasures of sensation are among these, *precede* desire, and hence cannot be set aside as simply consisting in its satisfaction. This does not imply that they have a peculiar quality which mysteriously elicits a desire and can be characterized independently of it. What makes my experience pleasurable is that what I experience in it is experienced as desirable. There is, I suggest, nothing to a pleasurable experience over and above this. Without having first formed a desire for her caress I *experience* it as something to be desired, and this is a different pleasure from the pleasure of getting what I already want, which need not consist in any experience. Finding myself enjoying something gives me a goal I did not previously have: it is not the satisfaction of a general desire for pleasure that I already have. Such a general desire can only be a desire that I will happen on *something* that I do experience as desirable. Thus, the pursuit of other goals is presupposed by, rather than presupposing, the pursuit of pleasure. It follows that the hedonist picture of pleasure as the end of all activity is incorrect.

One obvious way to bolster up hedonism is to regard desire as itself an uncomfortable tension, which is discharged through obtaining what is desired. The object is wanted, then, simply as a means of avoiding this discomfort, so that the absence of discomfort is what is always really sought. Freud, to whom we shall return shortly, held this view.

> We have no hesitation in assuming that the course taken by mental events is automatically regulated by the pleasure principle. We believe, that is to say, that the course of events is invariably set in motion by an unpleasurable tension, and that it takes a direction such that its final outcome coincides with a lowering of that tension – that is with an avoidance of unpleasure or a production of pleasure. (Freud, (XVIII), p. 7)

Behaviourist psychologists have sometimes held similar views, in the form of a 'drive reduction' theory of motivation. But such theories are quite inadequate. They confuse the desire for something, for example sexual intercourse, with the desire to be rid of that desire, which, according to popular mythology, can be achieved not only by sexual intercourse but by a cold shower. Yet we only occasionally seem to seek the object of desire in order to be rid of the desire, namely where we would rather not have the desire itself, and that is the exception, not the rule.

Is sexual desire a desire for pleasure anyway? The pleasures of even the least adventurous sexual activity are many and various. There are the pleasurable sensations from sexual contact, stimulation and orgasm which are localized in the body. To abandon oneself to these pleasures is to be voluptuous. There are also the pleasures of sense, of looking at and appreciating the sensible attractions of the one who is desired, whose pursuit is sensuality. There are pleasures too of sexual activity, as against receptivity, pleasures one might say, of venery. There are fleshly pleasures, of becoming pleasurably aware of our existence as human bodies, pleasures of carnality. There are pleasures of escape from an awareness of the facts of existence, pleasures of fantasy, and many more. I have noted the archaic excesses to which these various pleasures tend in order to emphasize how *specialized* an activity sex for pleasure is. Even when several pleasures combine, what makes them all *sexual* has little to do with what renders them pleasures. There is no obviously stable end of sexual desire, to explain the relatively stable fact that it motivates us. When it does, no specific pleasure may be in view. Mildly aroused or passionately desirous we act, and the motivation may be the same whatever pleasure we take in the result.

2.3   *Unconscious Impulses*

Freudian explanations

We do not think of our most significant social relations as undertaken for pleasure. To be told that they are, and cannot but be, seems to diminish them. Even if acceptance of a general hedonism preserved our preferences, it would change their character, since we do not naturally think of a casual sexual encounter and a long-lasting love affair, for example, as differing only in the amount of pleasure each may bring. Of course we hope for something out of love; happiness, we would probably call it, rather than pleasure. High-mindedly, however, we think of happiness as a possible by-product of offering our love, not the aggregate of pleasures we aim at in doing so. We think also of our love as at least sometimes aimed at the other's happiness, rather than our own.

Now even if this thought is not confused, it may be false for all that. Conventional pieties about disinterestedness and altruism may be applicable in some areas of human relationship; perhaps it is in the most intimate and passionate ones that they cut least ice. Are not these the areas where our motives are most unclear to us? More generally, might it not be the case that we are *unconscious* of the character of the desires that motivate us in love? If so, love may be only a species of sexual desire, all its apparent concern and consideration simply a tactic to achieve, if only partially, the aim of sexual desire. If this is pleasure, then, although we may be unconscious of it, it is pleasure that we seek.

It is evident that we have here a popular pattern for providing a reductive explanation of any relationship. All that is needed for applying it is a scientific theory of basic impulses which give rise to our behaviour, but which play no corresponding part in our ordinary thinking about relationships. What prevents us thinking in these terms is that we are commonly unconscious of these impulses. What does this mean?

It is important to see that explanation by unconscious desires is not simply a version of the accounts that Tolstoy and de Sade provide. Their actors are hypocrites or muddleheads; a stiff dose of the honesty and clarity that Tolstoy and de Sade prescribe is meant to put them right about their real inclinations. By contrast *intellectual* assent to the doctrine of unconscious motivation is not enough to bring us to see our own personal practice differently in a way that makes change possible. The fact that we are unconscious of our real desires is itself to be explained in terms of a theory about their origins, development and later manifestation. So long as this is 'normal', there is no reason why we should need to change our practice. If it is not, then to come to see it differently, after treatment for example, is already to change it in the light of changes in the desires that govern it. The principal point of the theory is not to affect our own practice but to bring us to understand the practice of others in a way that, as the agents of it, they do not.

This kind of view is, of course, closely associated with the Viennese psychiatrist Sigmund Freud and his contemporary followers like Jaques Lacan. It is worth sketching Freud's own view of sexual love, if only because those who offer a reductive account intended in the spirit of Freud commonly misinterpret him.

Freud held, as an inference from his clinical observations, that in infancy children have sexual desires directed at their parents, partly because it is they who, unwittingly, stimulate their erotogenic zones. Thus Freud has no doubt about 'identifying a child's affection ... for those who look after him with "sexual love"' (Freud, (VII), p. 233). As childhood proceeds these 'sexual' tendencies are repressed, so that the sexual character of the child's attitude to its parents is relegated to the unconscious. What is left behind is an 'affectionate current' (ibid., p. 115) of sexuality, inhibited from attaining a directly sexual aim, but continuing to motivate through creating sexual tension.

At puberty the sexual current is reawakened, its new aim being sexual intercourse rather than simple stimulation of erotogenic zones. But this needs to be accompanied by a directing of the affectionate current towards the object of sexual interest. Unlike de Sade, Freud regards a purely sexual relationship as unsatisfactory: 'a normal sexual life', he says, 'is only assured by an exact convergence of the affectionate current and the sexual current', (ibid., p. 207). 'The depth to which anyone is in love,' he suggests, 'as contrasted with his purely sensual desire, may be measured by the size of the share taken by the aim-inhibited instincts of affection', (Freud, (XVIII), p. 112). Because the sexual aim of the affectionate current is inhibited it is incapable of complete satisfaction. For this reason it can give rise to the 'lasting ties between people', which uninhibited sexual impulses would not create (ibid., p. 258).

Freud's view is, in fact, that *all* kinds of love and attachment are 'an expression of the same instinctual impulses; in relations between the sexes these impulses force their way towards sexual union, and in other circumstances they are diverted from their aim or are prevented from reaching it though always preserving enough of their original nature to keep their identity recognisable (as in such features as the longing for proximity, and self-sacrifice)' (ibid., pp. 90–1). Even these features, according to Freud, are manifestations of sexual instinct. Should someone claim to prefer a relationship characterized by them, but with fewer opportunities for sexual satisfaction, his underlying desires will still be sexual, albeit of the aim-inhibited variety. Freud regards this process as responsible not only for love but for all group formation, since it explains the behaviour of an individual towards any other who secures his devotion. He is thereby able to dispense with any other impulse postulated to account for social bonds, for example the so-called 'herd instinct'. The reduction of love and all analogous human relationships to unconscious manifestations of sexual impulse is complete.

Three points need noticing about Freud's account. First, it is an account of the sexual *character* of the apparently non-sexual aspects of personal relations, not simply of their sexual *origins*. This distinguishes these personal relations from activities which clearly result from *sublimation*. There, 'what was originally a sexual instinct finds satisfaction in some achievement which is no longer sexual but has a higher social or ethical valuation as a result of its replacing the original sexual aim' (ibid., p. 256). Artistic activity, for example, is held to be the result of sublimation. Second, we must not fall into the vulgar error of supposing that affection arises from the *frustration* of sensual impulses in adult life, so that love is seen as the product of a sexually repressive society. Freud emphasizes that repression takes place in childhood, so that the sexual instincts in the affectionate current never acquire the adult aim of genital sexuality which is frequently frustrated. Were this not so, it is hard to see why activities deriving from the affectionate current should be *unconsciously* sexual.

Third, although, as we have seen, Freud is a hedonist, his hedonism is postulated simply to provide a general mechanism for explaining motivation. Although he thinks the aim of an impulse is 'always discharge accompanied by satisfaction', (ibid.) this is only because he thinks that its producing discharge of tension and satisfaction is what explains why what is wanted, for example sexual intercourse, is aimed at. Thus if we are unconscious of the pleasure-seeking character of our impulses that is only because we are unconscious of their sexual aims. It is the exclusively sexual, rather than the exclusively hedonistic, character of love and other relationships, which, on Freud's account, directly challenges our ordinary thinking. The question we have to ask is how

such a picture threatens the ordinary explanations we offer for our social
acts.

Reasons and rationalizations

In Graham Greene's *The Heart of the Matter* the depressed colonial
police officer Scobie falls for a young woman, Mrs Rolt, who is brought
ashore after her ship has been sunk. The reader knows that they are
attracted to each other although 'they both had an immense sense of
security: they were friends who could never be anything else than
friends' (Greene, p. 145). Only when eventually they kiss do they learn
that 'what they had thought was safety proved to have been the
camouflage of an enemy who works in terms of friendship, trust and
pity' (ibid., p. 169) – sexual desire. Could *all* relationships of love or
friendship be like this, save that their exclusively sexual character goes
for *ever* unrevealed to their protagonists?

Freud's conclusion that they are depends on the claim that we would
not have manifested concern for the other unless we had had a sexual
interest in them. This is what allegedly brings out, as Freud's follower
Lacan puts it, 'the specious character of this supposed altruism, which
is pleased to preserve whose well-being? – of him who, precisely, is
necessary to us, (Lacan, p. 192). The suggestion is that our protestations
of concern for another do not give our real reasons for action, but only
a rationalization. A clear case of a rationalization occurs when someone
would have acted similarly even if the justification he offers had not
been available to him, as when the habitual bully slaps his wife's face
'because she is hysterical'. Yet Freud is not arguing that in this sense we
can provide only rationalization for our social acts, since if many of our
actions were not even *apparently* concernful we would not engage in
them. Nor can Freud be saying that concern cannot be a *sufficient*
reason for our actions on the grounds that we would not act thus
without the *additional* motive of desire. He wants to say that desire is
our *only* motive here. Yet one apparent motive, concern, does not
become *inoperative* simply because it functions only in conjunction with
another – sexual desire. To show that it is inoperative Freud would need
to show that its ultimate aim is, as Lacan implies, not the well-being of
the other but the sexual satisfaction of the agent.

Yet Freud must have great difficulty in showing this. The affectionate
current is, we will remember, *aim-inhibited*. Although the sexual impulse it manifests has a sexual aim, it is one the lover resists as something to be attained, contenting himself with 'certain approximations to
satisfaction'. It is not, therefore, a consideration that weighs with him in
deciding how to act, even unconsciously. Thus Freud cannot show that

the lover's reasons for concernful actions are a rationalization by show-ing that he acts to achieve an aim *other* than the one which he professes. The bestowal of concern is just what he contents himself with. What Freud needs to show is that the features of what the affectionate current seeks are sought *as* sexually desirable, albeit unconsciously. Yet this must surely be a difficult task. Certainly activities themselves non-sexual can take on a consciously sexual colouring when performed with some-one we find attractive. To generalize from these cases, however, to all those where we display concern for another, even in a sexual relation-ship, seems quite implausible.

Reflection on such cases does, however, suggest one kind of rational-ization into which Freud might have thought our ordinary justifications of concernful behaviour fell. While they may genuinely explain that behaviour they do not, perhaps, explain why we show concern to just *those* people whom we do. Our *choice* of lover, friend or colleague on whom to bestow affection and concern will, Freud thought, have an unconsciously sexual explanation, dependent principally on the mechan-isms for transferring affection originally shown only to our parents. Certainly, as we shall see, such choices are not easily explained in ways transparent to us. Yet even if the Freudian explanation of them is correct it does not follow that when we profess concern for those we choose we are only rationalizing our sexual desire for them. Concern is not 'spe-cious' just because it is directed at them and not at others in the same circumstances; for in giving reasons in terms of our concern we seldom purport to bestow it on anyone indifferently. That we have – or seek – a relationship with someone is a *reason* for showing concern for them as against others.

In fact, that something contributes to the welfare of a lover or a friend surely is a *reason* for wanting it, whatever our sexual desires may be. Why should we need to seek a *further* explanation of its being desired, any more than we do for the contemplation of beauty (which, of course, Freud regards as stemming from sublimated sexual interest)? There may perhaps be certian basic sources of energy that enable us to act from reasons, but they would not explain why reasons weigh with us. Only a much more radical attack on the everyday assumption that we do often act from desires that give our *reasons* for acting (such as is investigated in the following section) can, I think, tend to show that our social relations are explainable in terms of sexual instinct and the like. Other-wise there is no need to substitute unconscious sexual aims in explaining actions for which conscious non-sexual ones are adequate.

We should not, however, in passionless philosophical moments, ex-aggerate the evident reasonableness of what we do in our relationships, particularly in love. Freud is rightly struck by the cases where we would find it hard to justify the extent of our absorption with another person, the degree of our self-sacrifice. In *The Heart of the Matter* Scobie risks his job, his marriage and, Greene would have us believe, his immortal soul, for Mrs Rolt. Where this cannot be explained in terms of the agent's *conscious* reason-giving desires Freud seeks an explanation in terms of *unconscious* ones. That is why he seeks to show that I unconsciously view such actions as being, or leading to results that are, sexually desirable. It is under this description, he thinks, that they do recommend themselves to me as reasonable. Yet, far from undermining our ordinary explanations in terms of reasons, this *limited* attempt to account for apparently unreasonable actions presupposes it. It also, of course, extends the range of behaviour that can be regarded as done for a reason. In doing so it relies upon and so cannot undermine our ordinary grasp of what can count as a reason.

2.4   *Reproductive Strategies*

Schopenhauer and the will to live

In the preceding two sections we have looked at two ways in which the reductive view that love is but a species of sexual desire might be defended. In the first we investigated the hedonist theory that what gives us a reason for acting is always the prospect of some form of pleasure. In the second we saw how the theory might be modified to hold that it is the sexually pleasurable aspect of some outcome which *unconsciously* gives one a reason for seeking it. Both views strive to identify the agent's reasons for acting as other than the ostensible ones. But both are versions of a broader view that restricts the range of desires that could explain behaviour to those that can be thought of as *given*, as a brute fact about us, and thus not susceptible to further explanation. It is the view that, contrary to appearances, there is only such a restricted range that motivates the *reduction* of love to a manifestation of such desires.

In both the cases that we have considered the reduction can be regarded as *naturalistic*. That is to say the desires which are said to explain our behaviour may be thought to do so because they are features of our natural history. Hedonism, for example, is rooted in a mechanistic psychology which still has contemporary echoes: 'people are biologically "set" to seek pleasure and avoid pain', and 'this biological trait' is deemed 'essential to human survival' (Walster, p. 135). Similarly, Freud's view of sexual desire as an instinctual impulse locates it firmly as a biological drive. On this kind of view all human relationships are seen as aspects of our biological nature, and their essential characteristics are to be explained in terms of our biological propensities, for only the biological role of human behaviour is regarded as explaining it. If we have reasons for our acts it is because our goals serve a biological purpose.

The particular version of this naturalistic view which we must now investigate claims that, while we do perforce act from such biologically given desires, they do not give us *reasons* for our acts through presenting their outcomes as desirable, in the way that hedonism and Freudianism suppose they do. The *only* understanding of our activities and relationships they provide is one that shows how they are the working-out of biological mechanisms. The appearance of desirability is, at worst, a confused rationalization of processes that would go on without it; at best, a by-product of these processes, itself inoperative in advancing their ends. It is our biology which explains our acts, whatever we *take* the explanation of our acts to be.

The view is, as I have presented it, a perfectly general one. But, like hedonism, it has a particular attraction when we turn to human relationships like love, where, undeniably, biological mechanisms are operative in the formation of some of our desires. Do we here have an area where *only* a biological explanation will serve and ordinary explanations in terms of reasons must be abandoned? Recent sociobiological theories answer in the affirmative. But in order to highlight the philosophical issues they are best approached through examining their prefiguring in the work of the nineteenth-century German philosopher Arthur Schopenhauer.

Freud's theory of love and Tolstoy's in the *Kreutzer Sonata* owe much to Schopenhauer (though Freud apparently only actually read Schopenhauer after formulating his own). Schopenhauer, more radically than either of them regards our ordinary thinking about love as fundamentally deluded. He reduces love directly to a species of sexual desire.

> All amorousness is rooted in the sexual impulse alone, is in fact absolutely only a more closely determined, specialised and, indeed, in the strictest sense, individualised sexual impulse, however ethereally it may deport itself ... Now in this case the sexual impulse, though in itself a subjective need knows how to assume very skilfully the mark of an objective admiration, and thus to deceive consciousness. (Schopenhauer, pp. 533–5).

Schopenhauer sees that the lover cannot think of himself as simply satisfying his desire with someone: he must view her as someone objectively desirable, as having features which make his desire for her particularly appropriate. But this, he says, is a delusion, whether the features are thought of as 'ethereal' or as physical attractions. In the latter case these physical features may be thought to contribute to the lover's pleasure. Tolstoy, or more complicatedly, Freud, would say that this is what really explains the attactiveness of the beloved's features in either case. But Schopenhauer would not agree.

Schopenhauer is more radical than Freud or Tolstoy because he tries to show that love is a species of sexual desire without showing it to be the pursuit of sexual pleasure. Even the ostensible drive for pleasure depends, he thinks, on a *delusory* thought, concealing the sexual instinct from its possessor.

> As in the case of all instinct, truth assumes the form of a delusion, in order to act on the will. It is a voluptuous delusion which leads a man to believe that he will find greater pleasure in the arms of a woman whose beauty appeals to him than in those of any other, or which, exclusively directed to a *particular* individual firmly convinces him that her possession will afford him boundless happiness. Accordingly, he imagines he is making efforts and sacrifices for his own enjoyment, whereas he is doing so merely for the maintenance of the regular and correct type of the species. (ibid., p. 540)

Schopenhauer is able to treat the desire for sexual pleasure as itself delusory since he reduces all sexual desire, as we see at the end of this passage, to the workings of a reproductive instinct. 'The ultimate aim of all love affairs', says Schopenhauer,' is actually more important than all the other aims in man's life; and therefore it is quite worthy of the profound seriousness with which everyone pursues it. What is decided by it is nothing less than the *composition of the next generation*' (ibid., p. 534). But the importance of this cannot be impressed upon the individual; so the instinct is necessarily accompanied by the delusion that it is aimed at pleasure.

Schopenhauer's reductive account of love is, then, in two stages. The first reduces love to a form of sexual desire; the second reduces sexual desire and its accompanying inclinations to the reproductive instinct of members of the species. This is, for him, simply an aspect of the *will to live* – a universal will explaining all activity in nature. So properly speaking it is the species, rather than its members, which seeks to perpetuate itself. This second reduction enables Schopenhauer to explain the special features of love, its directedness towards a particular person and the unacceptability of a substitute, self-sacrifice to gain her and interest in qualities not purely physical. These arise, he thinks, from the (unconscious) aim of love as the production of the best possible offspring, inheriting their nature from well-matched parents. Love, Schopenhauer is implausibly claiming, is natural eugenics. To the obvious objections that not all love seems to have such consequences Schopenhauer has ingenious, though far-fetched, responses. Homosexual love, for example, allows old men a sexual release that does not result in the sickly and feeble offspring they would otherwise beget!

Schopenhauer's second reduction of the lover's desires to the reproductive instinct distinguishes his account sharply from Tolstoy's or from Freud's. Unlike them, he does not hold that what really explains the lover's actions is an aim (perhaps inhibited), which is different from their ostensible aim. As an aspect of the will to live the instinct is 'an irrational impulse, which does not have its sufficient ground or reason in the external world'. Metaphorically presenting this denial that our actions are really done for reasons, Schopenhauer says 'only apparently are people drawn from in front; in reality they are pushed from behind' (ibid., pp. 358–60). The kind of explanation appropriate to the lover's acts, as to all others, is not a reason-giving one, but one in terms of biological processes. It is not that his proffered explanation is a wrong explanation of the right sort, as a rationalization would be: it is the wrong *sort* of explanation. If we accept the account we can no longer find any reasons to act as we do, but, 'pushed' by instinct, we will continue to so act and fall again into the delusion of thinking we have reasons for our act. The account is, it seems one we cannot act upon. Is it one we should believe?

One question we can start by asking is whether the empirical assumptions underpinning Schopenhauer's view are soundly based. While his own attempt to explain social behaviour by a species instinct is a historical curiosity, his fundamental approach has been taken over by contemporary sociobiology.

The sociobiological programme

The programme of sociobiology is to extend to human social relations, like love, the kind of evolutionary explanation offered for those of other animals. The key aspect of evolutionary theory is that the genes of an organism that is successful in dealing with its environment are more likely to be passed down to successors than those of one less well adapted. This is how one must understand Schopenhauer's colourful talk of the species' 'will to live'. It follows from evolutionary theory that if our social relations like love are determined genetically then, since our species has so far survived, they are not at least radically maladaptive. They are not necessarily explained by a reproductive instinct, but as conducive to reproduction. It would, of course, be entirely fallacious to infer that if they are adaptive then they must be genetically determined, and to try to show that love, for example, is to be explained by biological factors by displaying it as adaptive. If it is indeed adaptive – which seems doubtful and difficult to establish – then that may be the result of cultural or social factors. There is no reason to think that individuals are genetically programmed to evince this sort of behaviour. People *tend* to wait for others to finish talking before speaking themselves. This obviously makes for efficiency of social intercourse. It would be otiose to infer that it was a form of social behaviour that was genetically determined. It is, however, hard to escape the conclusion that sociobiologists employ this form of argument.

E. O. Wilson, for example, argues that sexual love is 'programmed' as a form of 'pair-bonding' (Wilson, p. 140), whose evolutionary point is the reciprocal benefit to females of male support and assistance over a lengthy breeding period in return for sole sexual rights. Eibl-Eibesfeldt locates it in an evolutionarily acquired 'parental care drive' (Eibl-Eibesfeldt, p. 123) and Robert Ardrey in the imperative to share a territory for breeding (Ardrey, pp. 101–3). By contrast Konrad Lorenz believes that 'love arose in many cases from intra-specific aggression, by way of ritualisation of a re-directed attack or threatening' (Lorenz, p. 186). All exploit parallels in other species to argue from the utility of love relationships to their genetic determination. The variety of the accounts alone should give us pause. It should be noted that all give at most a modest place to sexual instincts. Love is not primarily a manifestation of sex drives, but of other factors which render our sex drives successful in transmitting our genes. Not all who appeal to such explanations share the cosy 'pair bonding' presumptions of these authors. It was a well-known night-club proprietor with a racy reputation who allegedly remarked, 'My sex life is not my fault: I'm programmed by my genes.' This is the message of sociobiology. What may seem like social relations entered into for good reasons are the result of evolutionarily acquired impulses. It is this thesis which is exemplified in the claim that love is but a species of sexual desire, when sexual desire is thought of as no more than a biological propensity. Substituting bonding drives and the like for sex drives does not affect the reductive character of these accounts. Do they successfully undermine our ordinary conception of human relationships like love, or, for that matter, friendship, parental concern and other social ties?

They might do so if the patterns of behaviour they explained were as rigid and unvarying as the tropistic courting and mating behaviour of birds. It might be that evolution had 'programmed' us with such routines activated by a combination of internal and external stimuli.

That would be the case only if our own mating behaviour was the result of an entirely specific propensity, genetically inherited. But our 'mating behaviour' is not of this kind. It is indeed so various that such a description seems artificial. It is, in many cases at least, intelligently adapted to its goals. Its goals are comparatively seldom reproductive: the objects of sexual interest are frequently infertile or indisposed to procreation. No wonder ingenious explanations are required to display such arrangements as adaptive. What is striking in humans is just the *lack* of reproductively efficient routines and any consequent evidence that we have the sexual arrangements we have because they are adaptive.

None of this tends to show that we do not act as a result of sexual and other biological drives which may need to be referred to in explanations of our behaviour. Rather it indicates the highly non-specific nature of the propensities to which they would give rise. The resulting constellations of behaviour, including those that typify love, are directed to certain ends: mutual understanding and happiness for example. The pursuit of these ends fashions our actions into shapes for which talk of evolutionary desires and adaptive tactics provide no explanation. If sociobiology were to explain our relationships it would need to be able to explain why we pursue these goals through them, as well as why they have the specific shapes they do. Otherwise affinities between them – the similarities of love and friendship, for example, – would be lost sight of. But that we pursue general goals of mutual understanding and happiness is not a biological generalization about us. It is not a general fact which the resources of biology are able to recognize. Biology is, indeed, not needed to account for the pursuit of mutual happiness, any more than it is needed to account for the pursuit of truth.

Let us develop the analogy for a moment. No doubt biology must account for the fact that, as members of the species, we have just the intellectual capacities we do: it may also be able to account for the fact that these capacities tend to yield true beliefs rather than false ones, since true beliefs no doubt adapt us better to the world. But this is not to explain why we seek the truth, as the desirable goal of our beliefs, since we do not seek it *because* it is adaptive – in some cases it may be better to live with a lie. Yet unless our beliefs were aimed at truth in this way they would not count as beliefs. Similarly, unless it was of a sort normally aimed at mutual understanding and happiness my attitude to you would not count as love. Goals such as these give us reasons for acting. The generalizations that sociobiology misses are those that classify actions together according to our reasons. In denying the reality of reason-giving explanations, then, sociobiologists are bound to fail in accounting for our relationships as we ordinarily conceptualize them.

To see this, suppose that all our behaviour can be given a biological explanation. It is fallacious to infer that our love affairs can be so explained. Yet that is the move Schopenhauer and the sociobiologists insist upon. The fallacy arises from failing to grasp that it is only under a certain classification that any event can be explained. 'Why did you murder your lover's spouse?' is not answered by 'My arm muscles contracted' or 'Such and such brain processes occurred', although these may answer the question 'Why did your hand, which was holding a knife, move in a certain direction, viz. close to your lover's spouse?' Yet the murder was not a separate event from the arm movement. It is, however, susceptible of a very different kind of explanation: what reason could someone have had, we ask, for acting under *that* description? The description under which the agent acts is the one under which we want our explanation of that act. But this description will not be a *biological* one, since as agents we do not normally think of ourselves as manifesting behaviour that falls under biological classifications. It follows that a biological explanation will not suffice to account for our actions. Biological explanations may run out long before we reach the level of description under which we act. No biological explanation at all, therefore, may be available for acts viewed as acts of love, in which case a reductive biological account is unacceptable.

Limits of biological understanding

We can now see more clearly why the kind of account offered by Schopenhauer or sociobiology is one we are so reluctant to accept. Such an account invites us to view the relationships in which we are participants and in which we have to find reasons for acting as biologists might view the behaviour of a different species. The reason that we cannot think of our love relationships, as Schopenhauer and sociobiology invite us to, is that we cannot in general think of ourselves simply as acting under biological descriptions. In particular, were I to think of another as simply the object of my sexual desire construed as a biological drive, I could not *be* adopting an attitude of love towards her. Observing my own situation as an example of biological processes would no longer be to feel love. De Sade grasps this point in recommending a *change* of attitude in favour of an overt expression of sexual desire. This move is not, however, available to Schopenhauer and the sociobiologists who regard the attitude of love as itself genetically programmed. Their account of it is one which, if it is true, we could not accept, for to do so would no longer be to have the kind of attitude which, according to them, we cannot help but have.

Even if we could change our attitude, à la de Sade, we would not simply be acting under biological descriptions. It may indeed be healthy to recognize our sexual impulses as an aspect of our biological nature, even though Tolstoy directs his barbs against 'the doctors – the priests of science – who deprave youths by maintaining that this is necessary for their health' (Tolstoy, (K), p. 126). His own attitude to the urgencies of sexual impulse scarcely seems well balanced. Yet to arrange one's affairs so as to accede to such impulses rather than resist them is not just to act under the description 'finding an outlet for instinctual drives'. It is also to act under that of, for example, 'doing what is believed to be conducive to health', and this is not a biological description. Following Oscar Wilde's dictum, 'Never resist temptation', is not, in any way that a biologist could recognize, acting like an animal.

It may, of course, be that, just as we have obvious needs for food and water, we also have a need for sex if we are to avoid some physiological dysfunction. Whether this is so is, it is true, something which it requires biology to determine. But if we then accept sexual desire as a reason for someone to act, that is not because we view his action as the outcome of the homeostatic mechanisms of the organism, which keep it functioning normally. Rather it is because the fact that someone *needs* something is, like his need for food, a *reason* for him to have it. We only speak of *need* when this is the case: psychopathic killers do not act out of need, even if they have, as psychologists describe needs, some physiological deficit giving rise to a drive state. Acting because of a biological need is not acting simply under a biological description. It is acting because it is better, other things being equal, to avoid some physiological dysfunction.

Although we cannot *accept* the sociobiological account might it not be *true* for all that? The only reason for thinking so would be if we thought that the only acceptable explanations of human behaviour were biological ones. In that case, the only understanding of ourselves as human beings which we could be seeking would be whatever was provided by biological science. Now it is important to notice that the claim that the only understanding of human beings is an understanding of them as members of the species *Homo sapiens* is not itself a scientific claim. It does not at all follow from anything that biologists may tell us about human beings. Rather it is a philosophical claim which could only be established by showing up other potential forms of understanding as bogus. If we could have shown, for example, that all our purported reasons for acting were rationalizations we would have ruled out one kind of alternative. But this, I have argued, would be no easy task.

Is it not, in any case, up to *us* what sort of understanding of ourselves we seek? Why do we seek such understanding anyway? Surely it is because we act in ways which affect each other and we wish to understand these acts. We wish to have other people's behaviour made intelligible to us in terms of desires for things which we can grasp as desirable or, at least, as intelligibly believed to be desirable. Only when explanation in terms of such reasons for acting runs out will we seek explanations in terms of biological regularities.

2.5 *The Obscure Object of Desire*

It is now worth asking why a pattern of explanation that appeals only to sexual desire – construed as a basic natural impulse – is so attractive in offering an account of love; why, indeed, this general pattern, appealing to similar basic impulses, is so tempting in accounting for all of our relationships. The reason is, I suspect, that, while the grounds of the desirability of many of our activities are evident, our reasons for love render its goal an *obscure* object of desire. A similar situation prevails in many of our relationships. We simply do not know what it is we want from them, what it is in virtue of which we find them desirable. Of course we can speak blandly of mutual understanding and happiness, but what these might come to in the context of a particular relationship is often quite unclear to us. We do not know quite what we are aiming for in seeking them; when a relationship seems to offer them we do not quite know what it is that promises to give us satisfaction.

In these circumstances it is natural to turn for an explanation of our behaviour to desires that regularly have this feature. Sexual desire can, at least frequently, seem the very paradigm of this kind of desire. I desire someone, and in two distinct respects what I desire can be obscure to me. First, what I want, what would satisfy me, may be obscure even when my activity presses on towards sexual intercourse; since what is desirable in that may not be clear. Second, what it is about the one I want that makes me want him or her, what is desirable about him or her, may be equally unclear. The extreme case of this phenomenon occurs when I can no longer think of what I want as desirable at all. Then I cannot think of my desire as giving me any *reason* to act. Instead I can only view my actions as caused by a desire which is identified in terms of the end-states typically terminating such activity. The identification of this state does not provide a description under which I think of it as desirable.

Following an old tradition, we can call desires which explain behaviour in a way that does not give the agent's reasons for action *blind* desires. The desire for food in hunger, the natural desire for warmth, the desire for a cigarette or for another drink, all these are commonly blind desires. Another drink is what I want. I fidget and move my glass around until you get me one. But this description does not present another drink as something I have a reason to get. Indeed I may, under that description, have every reason, and realize I have every reason, for not getting it. Yet I display a familiar pattern of behaviour leading to my getting it. Sexual desire can often seem to have this quality.

This is the way love presents itself to the hero of Somerset Maugham's *Of Human Bondage*, Phillip Cary.

> He did not know what it was that passed from a man to a woman, from a woman to a man, and made one of them a slave; it was convenient to call it sexual instinct, but if it was no more than that, he did not understand why it should occasion so vehement an attraction to one person rather than another. It was irresistible: the mind could not battle with it; friendship, gratitude, interest, had not power beside it. (Maugham, p. 587)

Phillip's own problem is that he cannot comprehend his own love in a way that clarifies the desirability of the woman he loves:

> When he lay in bed it seemed impossible that he should be in love with Mildred ... He did not think her pretty; he hated the thinness of her ... the unhealthiness of her colour vaguely repelled him. She was common ... and suddenly, he knew not why ... he yearned for her. He thought of taking her in his arms, the thin fragile body, and kissing her pale mouth. (ibid., pp. 424–5)

Viewing his situation from without, as it were, Phillip cannot see himself except as in the grip of a natural impulse. Yet this is a grip from which, in Schopenhauerian fashion, he cannot escape. He finds himself rehearsing the activities towards which he is impelled without any illumination of his motives being shed from within.

It is viewing sexual desire as a blind desire which naturally leads to accounts of it as a basic impulse explaining behaviour purely biological-ly, in the manner of Schopenhauer and sociobiology. Freud can be regarded as treating sexual desire as a blind desire behind actions in that our *conscious* thoughts of some object of affection do not bring out the mechanisms of sexual desire that motivate our affectionate acts. Uncon-sciously our reasons are to obtain sexual pleasure. In common with other forms of hedonism this seeks to domesticate the dark forces of blind desire by accounting for why they weigh with us in terms of a uniform pattern of reasons. This is implausible, as I have argued. Yet it

makes the right kind of move in attempting to make our actions intelligible to us by articulating what it is about what we desire that could be
thought of as desirable.

It is, I suggest, precisely the absence of any clear *thought* of the object
as desirable that leads to the desire for it being experienced as an
impulse. But experiencing it in this way is to experience the desire itself
as *undesirable*, as intruding unintelligibly upon my settled goals. That
is not necessarily to wish to be rid of it – to seek relief from sexual
tension, for example – but to seek to be led by what is desirable in what
is desired. This is to put myself in a position where I do have an
intelligible reason for acting. Without one, I cannot submit it to critical
scrutiny and rationally decide if it is worthwhile acting upon it. To
achieve this I would have to be able to *think* clearly what features make
what I desire desirable. The kind of understanding involved would be
quite the reverse of that which seeks to uncover blind desires behind
apparent reasons. To do that, I suggested, is to learn nothing relevant to
my situation as an agent exercising choice.

While Somerset Maugham formulaically invokes only blind desire,
revealed in moments of lucidity between periods of absorption in passion, a more perceptive novelist, Winifred Holtby, presents the practical
difficulty of making one's feelings intelligible to oneself. In *South Riding*
the progressive headmistress, Sarah Burton, confronts the conservative
school governor, Robert Carne, with whom she has fallen in love.

> She could not believe that last time she had seen him he had tossed
> moaning upon her bed; she could not believe she had lain weeping for him
> every night since then. She saw his solid body, his dark brown tweed suit,
> his bowler hat (who can feel romantic about a man who wears a bowler
> hat? she asked herself), the obstinate lines of his big handsome face. She
> thought, what a fool he is! She thought, he's just like Mussolini. (Holtby,
> p. 399)

But, after a fierce argument between them, the discrepancy between her
feelings and her view of him is, to a degree, resolved by a clarification
occasioned by this thought:

> He looked so comical, blazing down at her, his great jaw out-thrust, his
> bowler hat in his hand, that she broke into a bubble of laughter.
>   'Really, I do love your notion of governoratorial behaviour. You come
> bounding in here like a bucolic Mussolini and expect me to sit down
> meekly under your denunciations. And there's a ladybird crawling up
> your collar. If you had the slightest notion how funny you looked!' (ibid.,
> pp. 401–2)

To think of someone as comically vulnerable makes love and pity possible where before it was not (although *why* this is so requires elucidation).

Just as what is desirable about someone can become clear from a revealing thought, so, perhaps, can the desirability of our goals in sexual desire. Until we have a clearer view of that in general the project of reducing love to sexual desire cannot be properly assessed; although, I have argued, its attractions stem from the assumption that sexual desire is basic, given, not needing further understanding. The obscurity of what we desire in relationships is, I suggest, a product of our practical difficulties in them, of our problems in pursuing consistent but comprehensive goals. We think and act confusedly. In part, perhaps, this reflects the confusions of our culture and that is what philosophical reflection attempts to unmask. This chapter has tried to remove some obstacles to developing a usable account of what we aim at in relationships, obstacles which derive from questionable assumptions about the character and explanatory role of our so-called 'natural' desires.

Further reading

Two recent discussions of the relations between love and sexual desire are I. Dilman, *Love and Human Separateness*, chapter 6, and R. Brown, *Analysing Love*, chapter 2. It is worth asking what it is exactly that makes 'sexual' love sexual.

A good introduction to modes of explaining human behaviour is A. Rosenberg, *Philosophy of Social Science*, chapter 2, while R. S. Peters, *The Concept of Motivation*, deals with hedonism and Freudian theory. Freud's central texts dealing with love are 'Three Essays on Sexuality' and 'Group Psychology' (in Freud VII and XVIII respectively). I. Dilman discusses the theory in *Freud and Human Nature*. What pleasures *does* love provide? What distress does it relieve? Answers would contribute to elucidating the distinction between love and lust.

E. O. Wilson's *On Human Nature* is the classic sociobiological treatment. It is discussed in R. Scruton, *Sexual Desire*, chapter 2, whose own theory is interestingly criticized by J. Martin Stafford 'Love and Lust Revisited', *Journal of Applied Philosophy*, 1988. What, if anything, is *natural* about sexual desire? The notion of the natural needs close scrutiny. T. Nagel's Sexual Perversion' in his *Mortal Questions*, is worth reading here.

3

Power Struggles

3.1 Hobbes and Disharmony

The view that love is a species of sexual desire, regarded as a basic impulse, not only fails to account adequately for the caring, concernful face of love; it also fails to explain its darker tyrannies. In straight-forward 'uncomplicated' sexual desire one wants to be desired by the person one wants to have sex with. Being desired oneself both stimulates one's desire and smoothes the path to its satisfaction. But in love one's wish to affect the other's desires appears to become more generalized: one fixes on a particular person and wants them to desire what one wants oneself. A desire to control, to modify them to suit one's own desires can take over. This needs time to accomplish and is no doubt easier with one person than with two. The desire to *possess* the other can then come to seem an *essential* feature of love.

It can also seem a dangerous, even a damning one, rather than an accidental and perhaps disturbing one. When Goethe writes

> there is no sweeter bond of union for a young couple, whom nature has endowed with common sympathies, than when the maiden is anxious to learn, and the youth inclined to teach. It gives rise to an intimate and happy relationship. She sees in him the creator of her mental life and he sees in her a creature that owes her perfection, not to nature, not to chance, nor to any one-sided desire, but to a mutual will (Goethe, p. 164)

we may suspect the methods of the lover in Plato's *Phaedrus* 'whose law of life is pleasure and not good'. He sets about 'reducing [his beloved] to inferiority' (Plato, (P), s. 239). A mutuality of wills achieved in this way is surely even worse than the one-sided desire that secures an unwilling compliance might be. Evidently some desire for mutuality is necessary to love. But must this take the form of a questionable desire for possession?

The pessimistic answer is that it must. Love is on this view a desire for a certain kind of power with respect to another's acts that is exercised by inducing not fear but faithfulness. On this model the desire for possession need not be seen as an inexplicable extension of the desire for sex. Instead, sexual possession can be viewed as one instance of the desire for power satisfied, or sex seen as a key turned in the lock to secure one's possession. Sexuality can here be regarded either as the principal aspect of the person that makes them the object of the desire for possession or as providing the means whereby they may be possessed. There are variants on the picture. In each, however, it is notions like power and possession, drawn from the social sphere, not those of pairing and bonding, drawn from the biological one, that define the form of love relationships.

Here we need to contrast the conception of human relationships as inevitable reflections of our biological nature with a conception of them as the free creation of individual human wills. The former – naturalist – conception, does not need to deny the voluntariness of at least some particular relationships, although it tends to do so. It can hold that we enter particular friendships, for instance, quite freely; but our tendency to enter into any friendships at all is determined by our biological need for such relationships. This conception, then, emphasizes the continuity of these relationships across periods and cultures. It looks for the expected similarities, and has to explain the differences. And this is itself a questionable proceeding, especially when we consider relationships like sexual love, which, many scholars have claimed, is a limited and local phenomenon. If so, what sort of account of it should we seek?

A contrasting conception suggests that we view relationships as the product of individuals in conflict, each striving to secure his or her advantage. Without settled relationships these competitive interactions would be violent and damaging. Relationships of domination, subordination or rough equality develop to maximize overall benefit. Yet they are unstable, always prone to be upset by changes in relative advantage and necessitating the use of power to maintain them. On this view then, love will be a power relationship: a relationship in which one person has or seeks superior power in a particular area of life over another, who in their turn capitulates, maybe in exchange for other benefits, or resists, attempting perhaps to secure the power for themselves.

This individualistic conception does not need to deny a role to biological needs or instinctual impulses in the fashioning of relationships, but it is a different role from the one they have under the naturalistic conception. Such needs and impulses, it is claimed, do not have a *natural* expression in relationships; how they are expressed depends on how individuals choose to use their comparative power to satisfy their needs or impulses. The motive to acquire power can itself be viewed as an impulse rooted in our biology; but again how it is expressed depends upon the choices individuals make in particular circumstances of relative advantage. These may include biological factors – the relative strength of men and women, for example – but they will include others besides, including the scarcity or plentifulness of various resources.

The conception, then, is individualistic because it takes social relations to be explainable in terms of the behaviour of individuals. Its account of these relations is anti-naturalistic since it denies that there are natural tendencies towards social relations in that behaviour, that is tendencies that have a biological explanation. It may be described as 'voluntarist', in holding instead that social relations result from voluntary choices in pursuit of individual aims, so that social relations may change as a result – not necessarily intended – of these choices. It is conflictual in holding that people do not *willingly* abandon their clearly seen individual aims, when these cannot be fulfilled consistently with fulfilling the aims of other people.

The classic exponent of the individualistic conception is Thomas Hobbes, the English philosopher writing at the time of the Civil War under the pressure of the great social upheavals which produced it. He explicitly rejects the general notion that human beings are social animals, whose biological drives will lead them into harmonious relationships. 'It is true,' he allows, 'that certain living creatures, as Bees, and Ants, live sociably one with another ... and yet have no other direction than their particular judgments and appetites ... and therefore some Man may perhaps desire to know, why Man-kind cannot do the same' (Hobbes, ch. 17). Hobbes provides a number of reasons which are intended as empirical observations. Yet evidently they are observations of men in social conditions which may be the causes, rather than the effects, of the features they report. They serve in fact to elaborate the individualistic conception which Hobbes opposes to the naturalistic and which he thinks better explains their behaviour. Men, unlike social creatures, are 'continually in competition' for, according to Hobbes, 'Honour and Dignity'. Thus a man's 'Joy consisteth in comparing himself with other men' which prevents the common good from coinciding with individual satisfactions (ibid.). Any agreement between men is, therefore, 'artificial' – a result of choice – rather than natural. This is reflected in the prevalence of disputes in the conduct of common affairs which stem from fundamentally antisocial tendencies in men's behaviour. In a famous passage Hobbes allows that 'it may seem strange to some man ... that Nature should thus dissociate, and render men apt to invade and destroy one another ... let him therefore consider with himselfe ... when going to sleep he locks his dores; when even in his house he locks his chests ... does he not there as much accuse mankind by his actions, as I do by my words?' (ibid., ch. 13).

Hobbes believes that each individual pursues his own interests. What each takes these to be is determind by appetites and aversions arising in him naturally and giving rise to pleasure or pain. But since our appetites are never fully satisfied, 'the object of man's desire, is not to enjoy once onely and for one instant of time; but to assure for ever, the way of his future desire.' This leads to 'a perpetual and restlesse desire of Power after power, that ceaseth onely in Death' (ibid., ch. 11), since one can never be assured that one's present power will suffice to satisfy one's future wants. Power is thus a means to ends determined by appetite: our desire for power which places us in competition with others arises from the fact that in conditions where our appetites are relatively insatiable and our resources comparatively limited we need some power in order to live reasonably well. However, because living well requires peace between people we have a motive to enter into relationships in which we forego our claim to some things in return for the other's foregoing theirs. Such relationships, while they would be rational, are nevertheless inherently unstable unless enforced through the fear of superior power. Yet Hobbes, notoriously, gives no compelling reason why we should not seek to enhance our own power rather than submit to a superior one.

Hobbes has little to say about the small-scale relationships which are our present concern. It is significant, though, that he himself improbably attributes the 'concord' which is required for 'the government of small Families' to 'Natural lust' (ibid., ch. 13). Natural lust is, in Hobbes's view, that appetite which consists in the 'Love of Persons for Pleasing the Sense onely' (ibid., ch. 6). At this level then we do have a social relationship which is natural, arising from a supposed balance in sexual appetites in a couple, so that the use of power is not required. The example is instructive, since it brings out how the desire for power, for example over people, is secondary to the appetites. It is a desire for the means of satisfying appetites in conditions of competition, and consequently varies in its expression as the means vary in accordance with changes in the availability of resources and the distribution of power.

3.2　Conflict and Equity

The origins of love

The Hobbesian hypothesis about human nature can provide the basis for an analysis of *all* human relationships. 'For conflict theory', writes one exponent, 'the basic insight is that human beings are sociable' (he means 'tending to live in societies') 'but conflict-prone animals. Why is there conflict? Above all else there is conflict because violent coercion is always a potential resource' (Collins, p. 59). It is to avoid violent coercion that relationships are formed in which the threat of violence is organized and expressed in patterns of power and subordination. In the area of relations between the sexes for instance we need to note only that 'all human beings have strong desires for sexual gratification' and that 'males on the average are bigger and stronger than females' to conclude that 'without considering other resources men will generally be the sexual aggressors and women will be sexual prizes for men' (ibid. pp. 228–30). Family organization will, other things being equal, reflect the fact of sexual possession, conveniently overlooked in Hobbes's story of domestic concord. A personal, sexual relationship thereby becomes a *property* relationship, in which a woman concedes rights to her body rather than being taken by force. In a society where heads of households have some power to protect their property, control of women is transferable, made over to their husbands by their fathers. None of this, of course, need appear on the surface of the relationship. So that the ties which reflect power relations may seem quite natural – as to Hobbes – and do not require the explicit threat of violence in order to be forced upon their subordinate members. Indeed, the threat of violence may itself become institutionalized and made unavailable to individuals, leading to changes in the distribution of power.

It is on these principles that the emergence of romantic love, for example, can be accounted for, in a story that owes much to those nineteenth-century conflict theorists Karl Marx and Friedrich Engels: 'The most favourable female strategy, in a situation where men control the economic world, is to maximise her bargaining power by appearing both as attractive and as inaccessible as possible . . . since sexuality must be reserved as a bargaining resource for the male wealth and income that can only be stably acquired through a marriage contract.' The idealization of sexual relations that accomplishes this becomes 'a key weapon in the attempt of women to raise their subordinate position by taking advantage of a free market structure' (ibid., pp. 243–4). This idealization constitutes the phenomenon of romantic love out of ingredients that involve the marketing of sex to a more powerful partner.

Here in historical conditions of relative freedom from violence so-called equity theory or exchange theory can be applied, even if it is not applicable ahistorically. Human relationships like love are seen as self-interested transactions where, for example, less attractive partners must provide higher rewards. This may seem 'to re-define love as a devious power game' (Rubin, p. 82) but, the theory's exponents tell us, the search for equity or at least apparent equity in the transaction can explain both our choice of partner and the development of the relationship. What is distinctive about love is the role of sex as an exchange commodity, which is nevertheless not openly acknowledged as a separable item of exchange. Either because men's sexual desire is stronger than women's, as some post-medieval writers have thought, or, as more historically minded writers maintain, because women have compromised on their own sexual satisfaction, the provision of sex gives women bargaining power. Indeed since the control of resources that others want is a form of power, it gives them some power, so that a love relationship can indeed be seen to seek and to secure a balance of power.

Notice that in the Hobbesian theory and its contemporary developments in conflict theory, the power which creates relationships is not necessarily power *over* others, such as the threat of violence can give. The town council has a good deal of power relative to its citizens. It can provide them with, or deprive them of, services which they need but cannot easily provide for themselves. If it fails to satisfy them the citizens can use their power to vote in a new council. The town council has, however, few powers *over* its citizens. In contrast to national government there is comparatively little it can compel them to do. Similarly, the possession of mere bargaining power, in the form of sexual favours for instance, does not yet give a woman power *over* a man. That comes, if at all, when it can be used to make a man act against his better judgement, perhaps from the urgency of his desire for her. Hobbes and his followers have a tendency to move from ascribing relatively greater power to ascribing power over a person. But a desire for the former is not necessarily a desire for the latter. If lovers seek power in their relationship, they need not seek to dominate.

Rather, on the conflict theory account, they seek to promote their interests at the expense of the other's. They affect the other's interests adversely through the use of power. The fundamental case of this is getting people to do what otherwise they do not want to do – an exercise, as we may say (cp. Lukes, pp. 9–10), of first-dimensional power. But it can also involve getting people to confront choices in a certain way, to see, for example, the provision of sex as an exchange relation. The power to do that may be termed second-dimensional power. The conflict theory account of love which we have looked at sees it as a relationship in which the first-dimensional power of one category of partner – women – can be advanced, within a framework created through the use of second-dimensional power by men, who control the economic sphere.

Many questions can be asked about this conflict theory account of the origins of love, or of analogous accounts of the development of other relationships. How is an account which is couched in terms of *individual* motives – the desire to strike an advantageous bargain by exaggeration of the value of one's assets, for example – to be understood when applied to people who may have no awareness of being so actuated, who simply fall in love? They do not think of themselves as voluntarily conceding sexual rights, but of being overwhelmed sexually. Indeed, it may even be suggested that 'there is a formal contradiction between the voluntary contractual character of "marriage" and the spontaneous uncontrollable character of "love"' (Mitchell, p. 114). Well perhaps that impression is deceptive: it is remarkable how often in romantic novels the man the heroine falls in love with turns out to be the economically advantageous match. But how is a deception which might be possible at an individual level to be explained at a social one, that is, as a deception practised on men in general, and, indeed, self-deceiving to women? This would require a systematic discrepancy between avowed aims and actual motives analogous to that postulated in Freudian theory. What is unclear is how this might be induced by social conflict, particularly if its beneficiaries were the *less* powerful.

There are also, of course, questions about the acceptability of the historical account of love that is offered: does the account accurately describe the causal processes that give rise to love? That is, is the history merely consistent with conflict theory (as critics like Michel Foucault suggest (Lukes, p. 235)), or do the processes it delineates actually *depend* upon the theory's truth? Indeed is conflict theory really testable by reference to historical processes? All of these are interesting and difficult questions, but I want now to ask another: what light does the account of love's *origins* shed on the *nature* of love?

Romance and reason

At first sight, the picture of love as a power relation in which there is a struggle for advantage may seem to reflect merely a particular form that love can take. Certainly it is a classic form. The stereotypical love story of the nineteenth and twentieth centuries has all the features that conflict theory postulates as constitutive of love. Charlotte Brontë's *Jane Eyre* is commonly taken as a paradigm of the novel of romantic love. In it Jane, the governess who is the heroine, finds her employer, Mr Rochester, attractive but unattainable. Regretting the 'misfortune that I was so little, so pale, and have features so irregular and so marked' (ch. 11) she reminds herself that 'he is not of your order: keep to your caste: and be too self-respecting to lavish the love of the whole heart' (ch. 17). She notices, however, that the 'qualifications' of her rival, Miss Ingram, lie in 'rank and connections' but 'were ill-adapted to win from him that treasure' – love: '*she could not charm him*' [author's italics] (ch. 18). After a battle of wills between Jane and Mr Rochester, she agrees to marry him. She declines, however, to wear his choice of dress, feeling that 'his smile was such as a Sultan might in a blissful and fond moment bestow on a slave his gold and gems had enriched.' She warns him, 'I'll not stand you an inch in the stead of a seraglio ... so don't consider me an equivalent for one' (ch. 24). She cannot afford – and that is the right word here – to surrender her control of her sexuality, and insists that Mr Rochester 'should know fully what sort of a bargain he had made' (ibid.). Love is elicited precisely through the exercise of that control. Nor without it would Jane's sexuality be usable as an expression of love, of a free response to what Mr Rochester offers.

I have deliberately moved from emphasizing the features of an exchange that constitute the relationship according to conflict theory to speaking of the pattern of freedom and control that characterizes it. It is easy to object to conflict theory's picture of relationships that it is simply an empirical hypothesis about a relationship whose essential nature can be understood independently. As such, the hypothesis is open to numerous counter-instances. Many love relationships, even if we think only of heterosexual ones, surely do not exemplify the kinds of exchange it speaks of. That love is an exchange is disconfirmed by numerous relationships unequal in almost every way. That love somehow requires the rationing of sex is disproved by all sexually voracious lovers: that sex is idealized in love by all sagacious ones. A clear view of the value of what each offers the other is seen to be antagonistic to infatuation, not to love. Yet the theory is better seen as providing an account of the existence of a certain social form – the love relationship – than as an explanation of the existence of its instances. As such, it presents love as characterized by just the sort of relationship that is involved in any free exchange, in which the threat of force by one party has been replaced by the offer of benefits needed by the other. Agreement here is ostensibly uncoerced, so that each can regard the other as acting freely to comply with their mutual obligations under it. It is a relationship which, if not in every particular instance entered into only for perceived self-interest, is only *rationally* entered for that purpose.

It is this feature that is rebarbative about the conflict theory account. The value of a love relationship on this view is that of any successful venture carried out by sensible people in their mutual interests. It is when it is unilateral, irrational for one party, that it lacks value. Yet a romantic resistance to this account which goes on to locate the value of love precisely in cases where by these criteria it is *irrational* should not be dismissed too lightly. Jane Eyre's talk of a 'bargain' made with Mr Rochester is an ironical rejection of the conflict theory account, made within its own terms. The freedom of the parties to the 'bargain' is just that of admitting no *obligations* of exchange. Its value is seen not as the value of services rendered but as the value people can have for each other in a close relationship.

A romantic ideal here comes up against an ostensibly more rational conception of human relationships. What in the nineteenth century appeared as an exchange of assured security for sexual services by antecedently unequal partners appears in the twentieth century as an apparently more equal trade in social approval, emotional support, physical attraction and so forth. What leads from an initial interest to an established love affair, is in the view many social psychologists, *complementarity*: the ability of each parner to supply without undue costs the other's needs. On such a basis dating can be computer-programmed as smoothly as dealing on the stock exchange. And if, as we have no reason to doubt, such relationships do work, have not social psychologists uncovered their essential nature? Is love not an exchange of specific *emotional* benefits if not of more vulgarly physical goods?

The difficulty again lies, as with the view of love as a species of sexual desire, in the *reductive* character of the account, which neglects the participants' own view of it. The objection is not that we do not often think in terms of exchange and benefits when we love someone. I suspect that we do so a good deal more than romantics would allow that we should, and to do so would not be incompatible with being in love. The objection, however, is that such thoughts are not thoughts of love, that to act from them is not to act from love. Such thoughts capture neither the kind of concern for and hopes of the other which we have when we think of them lovingly, nor the sort of value we attach to a loving relationship with them. This is not to say that gross inequalities do not matter in love, that 'love conquers all'. If all that one partner was offered was opportunities for self-sacrifice, a real question as to why they should participate in the relationship would arise. But in so far as lovers demand equality they do so because the norms of the relationship prescribe a certain kind of equality, namely an equality in their rights to care and concern that prescinds from their antecedent positions of inequality. Equity does not consist, therefore, merely in the keeping of a bargain, which may be entered by parties with very unequal resources, but in equalizing the advantages and disadvantages of the relationship, even where no rational bargain to maximize individual benefits would prescribe it.

Here finally the weakness in the Hobbesian account becomes apparent. Our interests cannot all be specified independently of the relationships which, on the theory, are made to serve them. If we want love it is a specific relationship we want, not some further benefit which the relationship provides. We want the exchange more than we want the goods that are exchanged. The Hobbesian account falls down precisely from the feature that seemed to make it moderate and plausible: its appeal to appetites or fundamental desires as what relationships serve. It would seem then that the Hobbesian account fails in its generality since at least one kind of social relation – love – cannot plausibly be viewed simply as what arises from negotiation between individuals to serve individual goals that are prior to relationships. We shall return at the end of the chapter to defend this tentative conclusion against a powerful objection. First, however, we must look at a more radical kind of account which dispenses with the Hobbesian apparatus of antecedently given appetites, but still paints a pessimistic picture of relationships as power struggles.

3.3   *Nietzsche and the Will to Power*

Domination

It is a commonplace of worldly-wise conversation that love is the desire to gain power over a particular person. Hobbes's contemporary, the aphorist La Rochefoucauld, defines love thus: 'In the soul it is a passion to dominate another, in the mind it is mutual understanding, whilst in the body it is simply a delicately veiled desire to possess the beloved after many rites and mysteries'(La Rochefoucauld, s. 68). Mutual understanding, in accordance with La Rochefoucauld's precept that our virtues are usually only vices in disguise, is merely a cover for the drive to control another. No purpose is served by the desire. Indeed if the desire arose to serve an ulterior purpose it would scarcely be an example of love. But this absorbing and disinterested concentration on gaining control of a particular person is, cynics tell us, just what love really is. Yet is it plausible to impute this as a universal motive for love and what is it about people that might lead them to have such motives anyway?

In Edward Albee's play *Who's Afraid of Virginia Woolf?*, the protagonists, George and Martha, are locked in a power struggle that takes us beyond the competitive individualism of Hobbes and conflict theory. Martha, the daughter of a New England College President, has indeed made an unsatisfactory match with George, an Associate Professor of History at that college. George has failed to fulfil his promise and thereby deliver his side of the bargain. In the course of a scene in which Martha publicly goads him with recriminations, George dramatically breaks a bottle. But this only gives Martha the cue to continue:

> 'I hope that was an empty bottle, George. You don't want to waste good liquor ... not on your salary ... not on an Associate Professor's salary. I mean, he [George] would be ... no good ... at Trustees' Dinners, fund-raising. He didn't have any ... personality, you know what I mean, which was disappointing to Daddy as you can imagine. So here I am stuck with this flop.' (Albee, pp. 84–5)

She signals her freedom from obligation to him by attempting to seduce a new member of staff, Nick. She changes into a 'voluptuous' dress, though George observes, 'she hasn't changed for *me* in years' (ibid., pp. 46–7). Yet she tells Nick subsequently:

> 'there is only one man in my life who has ever ... made me happy ... George who is out there somewhere in the dark ... George who is good to me, and whom I revile: who understands me and whom I push off; who can make me laugh, and I choke it back in my throat; and who can hold me, and, at night, so that its warm and whom I will bite so there is blood; who keeps learning the games we play as quickly as I can change the rules; who can make me happy and I do not wish to be happy, and yes I do wish to be happy ... whom I will not forgive for having come to rest; for having seen me and having said: yes, that will do; and who has made the hideous, insulting mistake of loving me and must be punished for it. George and Martha: sad, sad, sad.' (ibid., pp. 189–91)

The battle of wills which in *Jane Eyre* concerns the striking of a bargain is here the heart of the relationship. What is at issue has moved, as it moves in the course of the play, from a concern with optimizing one's personal power in order to secure benefits, to a determination to maximize one's power *over* another person, while resisting their attempt to gain power over oneself. At the same time each is locked into the game (as the play characterizes it), where winning counts more than what is won.

The love between George and Martha typifies the 'battle of the sexes' proposed as the *definition* of heterosexual love by the nineteenth-century philosopher Friedrich Nietzsche: 'Has my definition of love been heard? It is the only one worthy of a philosopher. Love – in its means, war; at bottom, the deadly hatred of the sexes' (Nietzsche, (G), p. 267). Love is in Nietzsche's view essentially an attempt to dominate. It is a manifestation of everyone's restless desire for power and, for men at least, a direct and obvious manifestation: 'sexual love betrays itself most clearly as impulse towards property; the lover wants unconditional power over her soul as over her body, he wants her to love him alone and to dwell and rule in her soul as what is highest and most desired' (Nietzsche, (GS), s. 14). Sex is itself an instrument in the impulse to dominate; indeed, Nietzsche traces even the desire for sex to the search for power: 'Sexual stimulation in the ascent involves a tension which releases itself in the feeling of power: the will to rule – a mark of the most sensual men: the waning propensity of the sex impulse shows itself in the relenting of the thirst for power' (quoted Kaufmann, p. 222). So, by contrast with Hobbes, Nietzsche does not view relationships like love as a *means* to satisfy independently identifiable impulses. He sheds Hobbes's assumption of a detailed ahistorical human psychology in favour of an historically conditioned story of motivation. The impulses that we seek to satisfy in a relationship are simply the forms our desire to exercise power take in this relationship. Such relationships have no point except as expressions of the will to power. They are constituted by, and do not just arise from, a power struggle. It is in the universality of the will to power that we find the rationale of this pessimistic conception of love.

'The Will to Power' – with that phrase Nietzsche sweeps aside the biological explanations of human action and particularly social action offered by his predecessor Schopenhauer's invocation of the will to live. The will to live, according to Schopenhauer, underlies the particular impulses such as the sexual ones which tend to promote the continuation not of the individual but of the species. These impulses lie beyond the control of the individual whose individual will determines at most how they are to be satisfied in the prevailing circumstances. Nietzsche conceives the will to power quite differently. It is essentially individual. It is not concerned to promote survival ('Only where life is, there is also will; not will to life, but ... will to power' (Nietzsche, (Z), p. 138)), still less satisfaction or pleasure ('Man does *not* strive after happiness; only

the Englishman does that' (quoted Kaufmann, p. 270)). It is not the
desire for the means to such ends. Rather it is the desire for something
which is an end in itself. Other drives that may seem to posit different
ends are aspects of the will to power. The powerful personality has these
drives under full control. Such a person does not simply seek to enact
his or her will, but to maximize the scope for enacting it. So impulses
towards certain acts must sometimes be channelled into others. Here
Nietzsche anticipates Freud's notion of sublimation. But the impulse
that is sublimated – towards sex, for instance – still keeps its essential
purpose, the desire for power.

We can see here that Nietzsche's will to power is in essence no simple
wish to dominate others. Yet nor do I desire to dominate others just
to provide myself with the means of enacting my will. Others are, of
course, motivated by a similar will to power. Their wills necessarily
conflict with mine as each seeks to have their own way. I can have mine
only by limiting yours. At this point, if not before, it may be enquired
what the *power* that we desire, according to Nietzsche, really is. Yet if
we look for some substantive content to the desire, we should go astray.
That in fact was one of Schopenhauer's mistakes, in Nietzsche's view.
Rather, Nietzsche is making the point that to exercise the will is necessarily to display the will to power. To will that something be so is to
will that my will be done, that things are as I want them to be; and for
things to be as I want them to be because I want them to be so is for me
to have exercised power.

Stripping down Nietzsche's metaphysics to this fundamental point
gives it, we seem forced to agree, some credibility. Human relationships
can plausibly be viewed as constituted by the interaction of human wills,
so that their character depends on the relative domination of one will
over another. The subordinate partner may take themselves to have
made an advantageous bargain. Yet their choice of purpose – security,
for example – may itself reflect the subordination of their will to that of
others who feel no need of it.

Submission

With this apparatus Nietzsche is able to offer bold and insightful analyses of relationships, analyses which have subsequently influenced
existentialist thinkers in particular. The French feminist Simone de
Beauvoir, for example, bases her account of love on Nietzsche's. So far
we have looked at the relationship (assumed by Nietzsche to be heterosexual) only from the male point of view. But Nietzsche believes that
'the single word "love" in fact signifies two different things for man and

woman. What a woman understands by love ... is a total gift of body and soul, without reservation ... as for a man, if he loves a woman, what he wants is that love from her' (quoted de Beauvoir, p. 652). For a man, then, love is possession, for a woman to be possessed. Unable to compete for domination with a man, the woman achieves power by willing her own subjection. In this way she succeeds in doing what she wants because she comes to want what is wanted of her. But this imposes a demand upon a man that limits his freedom, namely that he should want something from her. As the Marchese complains of his wife, in D. H. Lawrence's *Aaron's Rod*: 'all she wants is that I should desire her, that I should love her and desire her. But even that is putting *her* will first' (Lawrence, (AR), p. 254).

Nietzsche appears to recognize the tension in such a relationship. The dependence of a woman on, as de Beauvoir puts it, 'this despotic free being that has made and can instantly destroy her' (de Beauvoir, p. 678) can generate hatred and rejection. As an account of the battle of the sexes it is compelling, and to this aspect we shall return. But is there not something too tidy in the interlocking conceptions of love held by the sexes in Nietzsche's account? Are they in fact neatly divided between the sexes in this way? (The role of self-renunciation was after all played by the man who paid homage to his lady in the medieval game of courtly love.) In fact the tension here goes deeper than that between partners entertaining distinct conceptions of love. It is surely a tension between distinct conceptions – or one might say between conflicting roles – that are required of *both* partners in love. The tension is, as appears from Martha's soliloquy in *Who's Afraid of Virginia Woolf?* a practical one. How can one both abandon oneself in responding to another and yet retain the means of control in the relationship which preserve one's self-respect? It is also, however, a theoretical tension which requires a philosophical resolution.

On the one hand stands the conception of love as the desire to possess another that goes beyond sexual desire. It is a desire to be desired by the other, but to be desired not just because one has some particular feature they antecedently find desirable. The lover wishes this responsive desire to be independent of the *beloved's* whims and to arise only because he or she desires it. And in general the lover wants the beloved's desires themselves to be within his or her power. (We can say in terms of our earlier terminology that he seeks to exercise third-dimensional power, the power to get someone to *want* to do something, even if it is not in their interests.)

Against this image of emotional tyranny can be set a conception of love as homage and obedience. It is the precise counterpart of – and required response to – the tyrannical role. 'To love someone is to desire whatever he desires for the reason that he desires it,' writes one contemporary philosopher, 'such desire is selfless, or altruistic, in that its objects do not directly connect with the lover's own other needs, longings, plans, ideals, with her beloved's; her desire is: for what he wants' (Fisher, p. 196). Although the choice of feminine pronouns suggests a Nietzschean story, this account is intended to apply to both sides of the partnership. Yet can it possibly be the *whole* story for each? As Nietzsche comments, 'if both severally made this renunciation for love, there would result, on my word, I do not know just what, shall we say, perhaps, the horror of nothingness?' (quoted de Beauvoir, p. 668). If each always gave precedence to the other they would find it as impossible to get through life together as mutually obsequious people find it difficult to get through doors.

Even if it is not complied with mutually, the model of love as obedience raises a dilemma: why *should* I desire what you desire? One answer is that it is just because it is you who desires it. I want to paddle in the sea just because you want me to. But this must not be because I expect rewards for obedience or punishment otherwise. That would scarcely be to comply with your desires from love. The problem is that *what* you want me to do may be something I can see no reason to do; indeed I may have reasons against it, a dislike of sand in my toes and of achingly cold ankles. Then what I want is desirable only because it is what you desire, and such a subordination of my will to yours seems pathological. The other answer is no more satisfactory. It is that I desire what you desire because what you desire seems to me desirable. This need not be because it is antecedently the sort of thing I would have wanted. Other people's desires can bring out the desirability of things previously neglected; the creamy smoothness of the surf may never have struck me until I grasped how it can be sensuously responded to. Yet, even if love changes what I view as desirable, it is that it seems so to *me*, and not that it does to *you*, which explains my desire. To respond thus is to respond for a reason, but not necessarily to respond frow love.

(Readers familiar with the philosophy of religion may recognize that the dilemma is exactly analogous to one encountered in thinking about religion – the *Euthyphro* dilemma, so-called after the Platonic dialogue which discusses it. Why obey the will of God? Either just because God wants it or because God wants us to do it because it is good. The former seems to dispense with conscience, the latter to dispense with God. The reappearance of the dilemma in a model of love as service and obedience is unsurprising, for the model trades on and parodies religious attitudes.)

No doubt in everyday relationships the dilemma need not be resolved, since the roles of command and of subordination can be adopted and reversed, slipped into for some purposes and abandoned for others, (although *how* this is to be agreed upon still requires an explanation). In *Who's Afraid of Virginia Woolf?* George's response to Martha's bid for domination is to 'break the rules' by 'killing' the imaginary son who symbolizes their union. But whether she can accept the game as George wants to play it is left – as we would find it in life – impossible to predict. In the next section we shall look again at the difficulties which flow from the dilemma of submissive love.

3.4 *Sartre and the Impossibility of Love*

While Simone de Beauvoir adopted Nietzsche's own story of hetero-sexual love as a relationship between unequals with counterpart concep-tions of love, her own lover, the French existentialist philosopher Jean Paul Sartre, argued that it was a more direct conflict between people sharing the same conception of their aims: 'the lover does not desire to possess the beloved as one possesses a thing ... he wants to possess a freedom as freedom' (Sartre, (BN), p. 367). He means that he wants to possess her as a subject of thought and action. This conclusion is more pessimistic than any of the conflictual accounts we have considered yet. The lover 'wants to be loved by a freedom but demands that this freedom, as freedom, should no longer be free.' This is evidently im-possible. If the beloved thinks and acts freely then the lover cannot determine the course of her thoughts and acts. Love is, then, only an 'unrealisable ideal' (ibid., p. 367). Neither party can get what they want from the other. The reaction of each to assert their freedom or their subjection equally frustrates the other. The conflict can find no point of equilibrium.

It is, of course, the dilemma which, as we have seen, confronts the submissive partner whose irresolubility frustrates the lover. Such a part-ner cannot freely, or, more precisely, rationally, adopt the lover's view of what is desirable just because it is the lover's. Nor if she adopts the view rationally, has the lover captured 'a freedom'. Either way what he aims for is frustrated. Yet, by contrast with Nietzsche's picture of the male lover as crudely dominating, in Sartre's *both* partners share this impossible aim of imposing their values while leaving the other free. A two-fold conflict develops: first, over whose system of values should triumph; second, over whether its triumph represents an abnegation of the other's will or an affirmation of it.

Iris Murdoch neatly sums up Sartre's view of love as 'a battle between two hypnotists in a closed room' (Murdoch, p. 65). Yet she is surely wrong to regard the account as abstract and unconnected with the facts of everyday life. It is easy to see both conflicts in the lives of individuals. The first is the source of lover's quarrels over whether each is loved for themselves or because they happen to suit the lover. The demand to be loved for oneself is to seek to be loved as a person in virtue of the features which give one an independent perspective on the world. But to value that perspective seems to require being drawn unconditionally into it, for to appreciate it only on the condition that it conforms to one's own provokes the complaint that one is loved merely because one suits the lover and not for oneself; because one conforms to their pattern, and not because of the attractions of one's own.

The second conflict surfaces in the rejection of the beloved's devotion as a satisfactory expression of reciprocal love. Responding to the lover's implied threat of the withdrawal of love unless he is accepted unconditionally, the beloved becomes clinging and uncritical, she then finds herself chided for lacking the individual springs of action necessary to a free commitment.

These conflicts are what structure the doomed relationship between the young, vulnerable Portia, and the older world-weary Eddie in Elizabeth Bowen's *The Death of the Heart*.

> She could meet the demands he made with the natural grace of the friend and lover. The impetus under which he seemed to move made life fall, round him, and her, into a new poetic order at once. Any kind of policy in the region of feeling would have been fatal in any lover of his – you had to yield to the wind. Portia's unpreparedness, her lack of policy ... stood her in good stead. She had no point to stick to, nothing to unlearn. (Bowen, (D), p. 128)

But Eddie is uneasy at her identification with his outlook. When she says she knows how he feels, he replies, 'you haven't the slightest notion how I behave *sometimes*, and it isn't until I behave that I know quite how I feel ... it's perfectly unforeseeable. That is the worst of it. I am a person you ought to be frightened of' (ibid., p. 232). And after knowingly hurting her, he reproaches her for the independent reaction he has evoked: 'I did once think I could tell you, even let you discover, *anything* I have done, and you wouldn't turn a hair. Because I had hoped there would be one person like that, I must have let myself make an absurd, quite impossible, image of you ...,' and when she replies, 'you are my whole reason to be alive ... I promise not to hate anything.' He responds, 'look here, shut up: you make me feel such a bully' (ibid., pp. 242–3). Eddie rejects Portia's voracious devotion:

'darling, I don't want you; I have got no place for you; I only want what you give. I don't want the whole of anyone ... life is so much more impossible than you think. Don't you see we are all full of horrible power, working against each other however much we may love? ... what you want is the whole of me isn't it?, *isn't it?* – and the whole of me isn't there for anybody. In that full sense you want me I don't exist.' (ibid., p. 259)

Taking such conflicts as these as the data that an account of love needs to explain, Sartre develops his view of love as essentially conflictual. The conflicts do not arise, he holds, because the partners deviate from the norms of a harmonious relationship. He does not treat a quarrel over whether one is loved for oneself and allowed a space to decide what one should be, as simply a *practical* problem of give and take. He insists that to demand autonomy and yet to be concerned at another's view of oneself *inevitably* puts one on the road to dominating them: *only* then could one be sure one's acts would be endorsed, although as the second conflict reveals *even* then one could not.

Sartre is right to reject the unanalysed notions of independence and the need for social approval that are the stock-in-trade of social psychologists. His own account of them stems from his analysis of what it is to be a human agent. It is to choose freely and that, he thinks, is to express the values one sets on things and which shape one's view of the world. This is an autonomy I cannot lose. But I find myself in a world of other agents whose views of me express their values, values which Sartre thinks, I cannot, as a distinct agent making different choices, grasp. Caught in the other's view, I find the world in which I act alien, no longer shaped solely by my values but by the unintelligible values of others. The only escape is domination or abnegation of the will. Unlike Nietzsche, then, for whom the will to power is an inexplicable basic drive, Sartre locates the desire to dominate in an account of what it is to be one agent among others. Relationships, although doomed to failure, are for him an inescapable reflection of this situation, whereas for Nietzsche we are, ideally, self-sufficient, not dependent on unstable relations of domination.

Later Sartre relaxed his view of the hopelessness of love: 'there is no love without that sado-masochistic enslavement of freedoms which I have described. No love without a deeper recognition and a reciprocal understanding between freedoms (a dimension which is missing in *Being and Nothingness*)' (quoted Howells, p. 38). Yet how is this 'reciprocal understanding' to be achieved? Two thoughts may strike us here. First, might not a unity of viewpoints arise fortuitously? Might I not find my soul-mate without the necessity for struggle? There might be a joint sense of purpose, Sartre could respond, but so far we have no basis for love, since this unity was not *achieved* in response to the lover's need for it. Second, might not a unity arise from outlooks *formed* by shared experiences, especially perhaps those of the relationship itself? Sartre would again object that this community of purposes did not answer to the lover's needs. It is a unity arising from contingent circumstance, not a mutual recognition of each other's values. Indeed, Sartre explicitly denies that the experience of a shared purpose – as of the crew of a boat, of friends or of a couple – can (as his existentialist predecessor, Heidegger, thought) be a fundamental aspect of their relationship, rather than something which needs to be explained in terms of its underlying conflictual character (Sartre, (BN), pp. 246–7).

The reason for this is not just that Sartre takes the values that we demand to be shared as nothing less than the agent's whole view of the world, rather than a few everyday moral attitudes and aesthetic sensibilities. He does have a deeply metaphysical view of a person's values as manifest in the entire way they live their lives, and thus something they cannot fail to act upon. We may well question this. But it is not the fundamental reason for Sartre's conflictual view of relationships. This is that the values we have are projected upon the world by the free choice of agents: they are not recognized in it. Sartre is, in other words, an *idealist* above values: their existence depends upon our idea of them. If, however, values were recognized in the world – if they had in some sense a *real* existence – then coming to share our values would be to share a discovery. No conflict need be involved, since the values we thereby adopt are neither yours nor mine. Since, on Sartre's view, there are no independently existing values, any attempt to share them will *inevitably* give rise to a conflict as to *whose* values, *whose* choices, are to prevail. And such inevitable conflict contrasts with the merely *contingent* domestic disagreements that dog relationships.

It is evident, I suggest, that this is not how we think about disputes on questions of value. The kinds of conflict between lovers on which Sartre founds his theory are under-described. What is resisted is not adoption of the lover's values, but adoption of them as values simply *because* they are the lover's, rather than because they recommend themselves as values. The lover is domineering if he will not expose them to the beloved's criticisms. He displays more interest in doing what he wants than in doing what is right. On the other hand, the beloved is slavish if she accepts them simply because they are the lover's values, failing to appreciate what it is about them that recommends them as values. But the conflict this may provoke is not irresoluble, since the beloved can be brought to see that the reasons he has for acceptance are not the right reasons. It is not a titanic struggle over whose values shall prevail, but an ordinary disagreement over who is right.

Sartre's individualistic view of ethical values is the root of his conflictual theory of relationships. If we accept it, we will indeed see nothing in ethical tensions but a clash of wills. Yet we do think of our relationships as answerable to shared norms of social behaviour and if the values they imply are only an illusion this itself needs accounting for. An example of such an account will be discussed in the next section.

It is worth emphasizing here, however, the radicalism of Nietzsche's and Sartre's view of the role of social norms in explaining behaviour. For conflict theory of the Hobbesian type social norms arise to resolve conflicts over the satisfaction of individual appetites. What norms are adopted depends on which groups of people are powerful enough to impose rules that tend to serve their interests. Behaviour in accordance with these rules, while the result of conflict, is not itself conflictual. By contrast on the Nietzschean and Sartrean view, social relations are constituted by conflict, since the norms their participants seek to apply simply reflect their own individual attempts to secure power by imposing their own values. In this picture the purpose of social norms is not to regulate the satisfaction of conflicting desires, but to reconstruct the desires of others in order to secure dominance. The apparent goal of social norms – the avoidance of conflict – is itself an illusory one.

3.5 *The Feminist Critique of Love*

Sartre presents love as an impossible relationship towards which people inevitably strive as a result of dual aspects of their existence: a desire for autonomy and concern at others' views of them. He does not regard the form of the relationship as itself devised to secure for the would-be dominant partner the other's subordination. It is simply the form taken by a clash of individual attempts at domination in this area. It would in any case be inapt to promote domination since it exposes both partners alike to the risk of subordination. By contrast, a view like Nietzsche's, which postulates complementary roles for the dominant and subordinate partner in love, does suggest that this conception of the relationship is itself a device conducive to securing power for the stronger party. If the notion of love is *itself* a weapon that some can use to dominate others by constructing relationships of a certain form, then talk of shared values that are accessible through it is beside the point.

This is the nub of the critique of love mounted by feminist thinkers. 'Love', it is urged, 'perhaps even more than childbearing, is the pivot

of women's oppression to-day' (quoted Mitchell, p. 103) or 'the
phenomenon of love is the psychological pivot in the persecution of
women' (Atkinson, p. 403). Love functions oppressively, according to
this account, precisely because it substitutes for obvious coercion an
unequal relationship which *appears* to answer to the desires of the
subordinate party. 'Since she is anyway doomed to dependence, she will
prefer to serve a god rather than obey tyrants,' comments Simone de
Beauvoir; 'she chooses to desire her enslavement so ardently that it will
seem to her the expression of her liberty' (de Beauvoir, p. 635). A more
recent feminist characterizes this as 'a special psycho-pathological state
of fantasy . . . this pathological condition, considered the most desirable
state for any woman to find herself in, is what we know as the phenomenon of love' (Atkinson, ibid.).

Now, so far, responsive love may still seem an inevitable condition in
the face of sexual domination resulting from psychological processes of
the sort that Nietzsche diagnosed. Through them the subordinate partner retains at least an impression of the power to do what he or she
wishes. Such a view would not imply, as Nietzsche does, that women
are naturally subordinate; only that whoever is subordinate will naturally react in this manner. But the characteristic feminist position is not
this. It is not that a change in relative power is required *before* the
conception of love as 'the most desirable state' can be unseated. Rather
it is that an attack on the conception can itself affect the balance of
power. And this presupposes that love is an *optional* response to sexual
domination, and one that is made only by those who do not grasp the
illusion which it involves. The charge against love is not just that it is
not in women's interests, it is that there is nothing more to love than a
relationship grounded in male dominance which is deceptively clothed
in putative benefits to women. Stripped of this clothing nothing we
could want to call 'love' would remain.

This position, then, does not place us in the intolerable situation of
inevitably succumbing to illusion. It explains our inclination to reject
the account of love in terms of conflict and domination as arising from a
false picture of the relationship which is, nonetheless, a picture comfort-
ing to the powerless and hence advantageous to the powerful. A clear-
sighted analysis of the relation between male lover and female beloved
will reveal the inequality of the relation. Then the comparative benefits
and disbenefits can be truly assessed. Even if, as the version of conflict
theory we looked at has it, romantic love was originally advantageous to
women in circumstances of economic insecurity, the somewhat more
equitable economic arrangements of the present day cancel its advantages. So seen, the feelings that surround the love relationship will

disappear – the sense of worth that comes from being attractive to a lover will be seen to represent a grotesque over-valuation, the sense of security in submitting to another's will a fatal paralysis of one's own, the sense of longing for an ideal happiness escapism from the day-to-day task of getting what satisfaction from life one can.

The mechanism whereby the illusion is propagated involves the projection upon the relationship of values that serve male interests, rather than the interests of men and women equally. As a result it can be *taken* to be a roughly equal relationship in terms of the realization of the values made available to each party. The dependent member, for example, can be grateful for the care and concern which is received and sympathize with the dominant one over the responsibility it imposes, regarding this as a fair exchange for her relative lack of self-determination. So far, it seems, the Sartrean picture of the victory of the dominant party's values prevails, albeit accounting now not for the shape of individual relationships, but for their prevailing social forms. But, by an ironic twist, women are made to feel themselves the *source* of these values. Invoking the role of the knight's mistress in courtly love, the nineteenth-century thinker John Ruskin writes of 'woman's true place and power' like this:

so far as she rules, she must be right, or nothing is. She must be enduringly, incorruptibly good; instinctively, infallibly wise – wise, not for self-development, but for self-renunciation: wise, not that she may set herself above her husband, but that she may never fail from his side. (Ruskin, p. 60)

This image of the naturally coercive male directed (and domesticated) through the love of a female moral guide bolsters the fragile self-esteem of the relatively weak, through the kind of process noted by Nietzsche.

I have lingered over this phenomenon because it brings out some features characteristic of *ideological* conceptions of relationships. 'Ideology', said Friedrich Engels, Karl Marx's friend and collaborator, 'is a process accomplished by the so-called thinker but with a *false consciousness*. The real motives impelling him remain unknown to him otherwise it would not be an ideological process at all ...' (Selsam, p. 214). Ideology characteristically disguises what its proponents *really* regard as worthwhile. This, however, can be ascertained by enquiring whose interests it serves, who actually benefits from the holding of ideological conceptions. For the theory of ideology regards those who occupy dominant positions as able to legitimize them by the creation of ideological conceptions (thereby acquiring second- and third-dimensional power). Thus the prevalence of such conceptions is explained by the particular forms that social relations of power and subordination have taken at different times and places.

We need to ask, then, if conceiving of a relationship as love is itself ideological, a product of false consciousness which disguises conflict as mutual concern and so forth. That depends, of course, on what conceiving of something as love amounts to. But only if our concept of love was that of a relationship *essentially* rooted in conflict would this conclusion follow. We have, however, already noted the implausibility of such accounts, for example of an account that characterizes love as an exchange of benefits between competing individuals. It is hard to see, therefore, that the concept of love itself is ideological. Rather, it is the inadequate conceptions which we have criticized that, by representing love as an agreed exchange of benefits, run the risk of ideological falsification. It is to these, not to the concept of love itself, that the feminist critique should properly be directed.

This is not to say that the concept of love finds a satisfactory expression in any contemporary social institution. To the extent to which it evidently does not, the feminist critique of love is justified. Like other social relations, love is the product of particular kinds of human interaction. Perhaps these are, always or only at particular times and places, irremediably competitive so that relations dependent upon other norms than free exchange, for example, are impossible. It needs to be said, however, that what social relations there are is affected by how their participants conceive of them. It is not clear, therefore, that we are entitled, as the theroy of ideology requires, to a notion of the *real* social relations which underlie and give rise to these conceptions, whether false (and in this sense ideological) or not. If only competitive relations existed, however, the conclusion to draw would not be that love is really an attempt at exploitation: it would be that love, if it does depend on non-competitive norms, is itself not possible.

We need to notice here the possibility of *moral* criticism of the social relations which people count as love under conditions of inequality. That is surely the reason for the feminist critique. It is that these relations are inequitable, demeaning, destructive of individuality. Yet why should we suppose that this is a criticism of the relationship which we call love, rather than of distortions or travesties of it? Surely the latter is more likely. We believe that love should be equitable, uplifting, fulfilling, not just because of a false ideological conception of love. We believe it should be so because we have normative expectations of it as a relationship within which a reciprocated interest in each other's individuality centred on sexual attraction can develop. Such a relationship seems good in itself, and is damaged by the suppression of individuality or the barriers to intimacy raised to prevent it. What permits us to claim a concept of love that is not just an ideological cover for domination is, indeed, that our concept has the resources for a critique of such domination as currently occurs. Even if such domination entirely outweighs whatever benefits love should bring we know what sort of relationship love *should* be, and what it might be in more favourable circumstances.

Indeed, we can, I think, go further and say that we have a concept of love that gives us a reason for wanting such relationships for ourselves and others. The benefits they bring are to be judged – as are the apparent benefits that a delusive ideology promises – by reference to judgements about what constitutes a good life. It is to the role of relationships in this ethical context to which we shall now turn.

Further reading

Hobbes's view of human nature in the *Leviathan* Pt I was attacked from the first, e.g. in Bishop Butler's *Sermons* I. Who was right? How can we tell? Randall Collins's *Conflict Sociology*, chapter 5, develops an account of love as a power relation. Useful reflections on power are to be found in S. Lukes (ed.) *Power*.

Nietzsche's views are widely scattered in his work. W. Kaufmannn's *Nietzsche*, especially chs 6–9, is still the best guide. A conversation between Schopenhauer and Nietzsche on the nature of love would be interesting to imagine.

Sartre's account of love in *Being and Nothingness* III. 3. i. is interestingly criticized by R. L. Taylor, 'Sexual Experiences', *Proceedings of the Aristotelian Society*, 1967. Is the kind of union whose possibility Sartre denies exemplified in the love between Catherine and Heathcliff in Emily Brontë's *Wuthering Heights*?

The seminal feminist text is Simone de Beauvoir, *The Second Sex*. Much recent feminist thought has developed the notion that sex roles are 'constructed', as found in M. Foucault, *The History of Sexuality*. See Rosalind Coward, *Female Desire*. What connection, if any, is there between sex roles and sexual relationships? Does homosexual love presuppose a heterosexual norm?

4

Loving Friends

4.1 *The Aesthetics of Love*

Beauty

'Love has always been for me', wrote Stendhal, the great French novelist, 'the most important, almost the only thing' (quoted Maurois,
p. 107). He means that it was for him almost the only *worthwhile* thing.
If such sentiments exaggerate, they are not wholly false. We value our
personal relationships in a way evident not only from our conception of
their importance but from the consequential shape they give our lives.
We may be able to revise our estimate of that value somewhat; we
cannot utterly discount it. Or at least, we cannot discount the value of
relationships without radically changing – if that were possible – our
attitude to our lives. For that attitude involves thinking of our relationships in terms of fulfilment and disappointment, security or loss. And
these presuppose the notion of certain relationships as worth having,
to be rejoiced in when had or grieved over when gone. Our sense of the
shape of our lives is determined by such thoughts of what is valuable
gained or lost, by contrast with thoughts simply of what seems agree-
able and what does not. Recurrent heartbreak can give shape to one's
life in a way that recurrent indigestion cannot.

We have to ask, then, in what the value of relationships can consist if
we are to have an explanation of our relationships that we, as participants in them, can accept. I have argued that the accounts of the
preceding two chapters are of the wrong sort to accomplish this. They
cannot, for example, explain the intrinsic value that is essential to love.
What other kind of explanation might we have?

It is natural to turn to the great Greek philosopher Plato for an answer to this question. It is to Plato, after all, to whom we probably owe the high estimation that sexual love has enjoyed in the Western world, at least since Plato's works were rediscovered in the Renaissance. We may expect from him, then, an account of the value of love which provides reasons for engaging in it which justify this estimation. But since Plato's views have passed into current thinking, they have also affected the practice of love, influencing the aims that lovers pursue in it.

In the *Symposium* Plato contrives a debate on the nature of love. One of the speakers, Agathon, brings their discussion to just the point that ours has reached by remarking that 'the previous speakers, instead of praising the god Love, or unfolding his nature, appear to have congratulated mankind on the benefits which he confers upon them. But I', he continues, 'would rather praise the god first, and then speak of his gifts' (Plato, (S), 194–5). In other words he wants to bring out what it is about love that makes its possession a *good*, something worth wanting.

Agathon's target is, in part, the comic playwright Aristophanes, who has just spoken in the dialogue. Aristophanes puts forward an explanation of love which denies the lover any *reason* for his actions, any conception of what he is engaged in as worthwhile. Thus lovers

> will pass their whole lives together; yet they could not explain what they desire of one another. For the intense yearning which each of them has towards the other does not appear to be the desire of lover's intercourse, but of something else which the soul of either evidently desires and cannot tell, and of which she has only a dark and doubtful presentiment. ((S), 192)

Aristophanes devises a fable to explain this obscure desire; it is, he says, that lovers are 'seeking for their other half', separated from it in the primeval past. This idea, in less mythic form, is still sometimes mooted today, surfacing in colloquial references to one's 'better half'. It influences the notion that lovers are looking for someone with *complementary* qualities – qualities which they themselves lack but which make the other compatible with them, so that together they form an harmonious unity. But the question that needs to be asked is what *reason* one has for seeking such a partner. For it is only if the other's qualities were *good* qualities, or if the qualities of the resulting couple were overall good qualities, that one would have any *reason* for pairing off with them. And this is precisely the point that needs making against equity theory and the like with their talk of a search for someone with qualities that make another compatible with me; for qualities like this, which are relative to my idiosyncrasies, are not as yet ones that make another person *worth* wanting. Thus as we have seen, *why* I should want someone under such a description is as yet obscure to me.

This kind of criticism cannot be levelled directly at the suggestion which Agathon makes, and which Socrates takes up, that love is of the beautiful: the possession of beauty is the possession of the good, which itself constitutes happiness: 'nor is there any need to ask why a man desires happiness; the answer is already final' ((S), 205). While this account covers love of anything whatever, it is acknowledged that only those who are affected by what we have called 'sexual love' are said 'to love or to be lovers'. That something is beautiful *is* a reason for wanting it. But does this desire really characterize sexual love? Can it explain the kind of importance we attach to it?

It is often claimed that what distinguishes sexual love from 'mere' sexual desire is its focus on the beauty of the beloved. This arouses emotion rather than immediate desire, feelings of trembling fascination rather than confident predilection. This kind of attraction is phenomenologically distinct from a directly sexual one. Some theorists (e.g. Grant, pp. 14–26) claim it to be an essentially non-appetitive attraction, only contingently linked to the aims of sexual appetite, although thought of as a component of ordinary sexual interest. Love is characterized by just this kind of attraction. Its value may be gauged from the fact that these feelings are 'like the feelings associated with the appreciation of art, and especially of music'. The value of love, on this account, is that of a kind of aesthetic experience. It derives from the value of the *beloved*, which is an *aesthetic* value, in just the same way that the value of listening to music derives from the value of the music, though the value of the music can be appreciated only through listening to it. So too, it is suggested, the value of a love relationship lies in the value of the opportunity it affords for appreciating the beauty of the beloved, which, perhaps, can only be fully appreciated within it.

This comparison between love and aesthetic experience should make us wary. It has been a commonplace of philosophical aesthetics since the eighteenth century, and in particular since Kant, that the experience of beauty is detached, disinterested, unconnected with our pre-existing desires and purposes. It consists, on this view, in the pleasure of contemplation, not of the satisfaction of some desire. It is understandable, then, that it should be contrasted with sexual desire as a motive in love. Yet surely the comparison is suspect at two levels. First, the emotional detachment we may feel before a work of art that inspires us – Titian's great *Bacchus and Ariadne*, say – is not at all the kind of distance from immediate desire that we may feel in ordinary life when suddenly struck by a beloved's beauty. In looking at the picture our imaginative involvement in the scene – Ariadne's dramatic meeting with the disturbingly beautiful young god – is checked and contained within the swaying rhythms of the painting. We are not to suppose, by contrast, that Ariadne's own state of mind preserves any such equilibrium as ours. The beauty of another *is* disturbing; it arouses, it does not check, emotion. And we *are* moved, involved; it is no merely imagined feeling, held apart from our actual ones, that can account for the distancing effect of someone's beauty. The lover's state of mind is not a contemplative aesthetic one, even if it is free of immediate desire. What distances the lover from the aim of desire is, in fact, an absorption in the beloved's beauty that excludes effective thought in the immediate service of that aim. It is also that no *single* aim is presupposed in the reactions that constitute the lover's response to beauty. But this is not to say that sexual aims are not among them. Indeed, it is hard to see how the lover's gaze would be possible without some sexual reaction, which is what the theory contrasts it with.

This brings us to the second point at which the comparison between aesthetic contemplation and a lover's gaze is prone to mislead us. We do not need to be as reductive as Nietzsche to appreciate his criticism of Schopenhauer in Kantian mood.

> Of few things does Schopenhauer speak with greater assurance than he does of the effect of aesthetic contemplation: he says of it that it counteracts *sexual* 'interestedness' like lupulin and camphor; he never wearied of glorifying in this liberation from the 'will' as the great merit of the aesthetic condition .... Stendhal, a no less sensual but more happily constituted person than Schopenhauer, emphasizes another effect of the beautiful: 'the beautiful *promises* happiness'; to him the fact seems to be precisely that the *beautiful arouses the will* ('interestedness'). ((G), pp. 104–5)

The point that Nietzsche notices is that aesthetic contemplation itself requires a *reaction*, an engagement of interest. Nietzsche locates this in Schopenhauer's case in a self-concealed sexual interest, but this is not necessary to his observation. What is important is that the reaction required to beauty in art, a reaction of pleasure and excitement, of absorption in the object of the senses, is the *kind* of reaction required for sexual desire. The aesthetic attitude itself is not disinterested and disembodied in the way that the theory requires.

The contrast between sexual desire and love, where the latter is associated with the disinterested contemplation of beauty, is ill drawn. Neither love nor the contemplation of beauty are sufficiently isolated from desire to make the contrast work; though the way in which aesthetic contemplation can be emotionally detached contrasts with the passionate involvement of love.

Plato himself, however, does not support his claim that love is a *desire* for the beautiful with this kind of contrast between it and sexual desire. Indeed he thinks of sexual desire itself as a species of the desire for the beautiful – inverting Nietzsche's reduction of the latter to the former. He does so because only then can he see sexual desire itself as intelligible to us, giving us a reason for our sexual acts by presenting them as aimed at securing something desirable, namely beauty.

The eye of the beholder

We may wonder, however, whether a desire for beauty can really explain the nature and value of sexual love, and this for two reasons. First, we may wonder whether, if beauty is detected only through an *affective* – a *felt* – reaction to what is deemed beautiful, it can be regarded as a property of the object that gives us a *reason* for wanting it. Our wanting it in this particular way is, it may seem, all that there is to recognizing that it is beautiful. But this objection cannot be sustained. That I have to be *able* to react appropriately in order to detect beauty does not imply that my reactions cannot be assessed as right or wrong, justified by something's beauty or unjustified owing to its absence. In particular the reactions of others provide a yardstick against which I can compare my own. Agreement in our reactions seems to be required for objectivity in aesthetic judgement, and objectivity is required if we are to think of a thing's beauty as giving us a reason for wanting it.

Yet this brings us directly to the second objection. Assuming that the ascription of beauty to works of art were an objective matter, can this seriously be claimed about the lover's ascription of beauty to the beloved? Surely there are as many different reactions to personal beauty as there are lovers to ascribe it. There is, luckily it may be said, little agreement in what people find compellingly beautiful in their beloved. But then the foregoing defence of beauty as giving a reason for desire seems to collapse. Trying to rescue it by emphasizing the agreement that does exist also leads to problems, of the sort noticed by Toni Morrison in *The Bluest Eye*. Describing the experience of a poor black girl in Ohio, Pauline, the novelist comments:

> Along with the idea of romantic love, she was introduced to another – physical beauty. Probably the most destructive ideas in the history of human thought. Both originated in envy, thrived in insecurity, and ended

in disillusion. In equating physical beauty with virtue, she stripped her mind, bound it and collected self-contempt by the heap. She forgot lust and simple caring for. She regarded love as possessive mating, and romance as the goal of the spirit .... She was never able, after her education in the movies, to look at a face and not assign it some category in the scale of absolute beauty, and the scale was one she absorbed in full from the silver screen .... It was really a simple pleasure, but she learned all there was to love and all there was to hate. (p. 113)

If the lover's interest is focused on physical beauty, and the standards for physical beauty are fixed by the cinema, then the resulting relationship, it is suggested, will lack goals that are internal to it rather than imposed by an unrealistic stereotype. One might add that it will thereby lack the *personal* character required for love, by contrast with infatuation: the criteria for choice are insufficiently rooted in an individual response rather than in a general cultural one.

Yet this observation begins to provide an answer to the objection to regarding the desire for beauty as essential to explaining the value of love. The objection was that beauty needs to be an objective feature of things to give us a reason for wanting them; but that the beauty lovers ascribe to each other is not an objective feature of them, only a projection of their mutual attraction; and so it provides no reason for the desire and hence no value in its satisfaction. The reply to the objection must be that the beauty of the beloved *can* be objective, even if it is not generally agreed to. For not everyone is moved to the same extent by different features that conduce to beauty, even though we can generally be brought to see what others find more compellingly beautiful than we do.

This enables us to see the importance of an *individual* response to personal beauty. For there are standards of appropriateness in our reactions to another's physical presence other than, and possibly in conflict with, agreement with the reactions of people generally. They are standards which demand that our reactions be heartfelt, rather than in tune with the reactions of people generally. To produce what simply seems to others the right reaction is evidently inappropriate in responding to another with love. Yet it by no means follows that there are *no* standards of appropriateness in our reactions whereby misjudgements can be corrected. We can for example mistake as individually beautiful someone who is evocative of a former love or who arouses only sexual desire or compassion. In such cases we mistake for a property that exists independently of our reactions, as beauty does, what is simply the product of these reactions. But these mistakes are correctible as we become clearer about the nature of our reactions or about what they are reactions to. Thus there is no reason to think that we are not responding to objective features, even though, as a matter of fact, they are not features which most people are able to discern as beautiful.

I am inclined to think, then, that, suitably qualified, we should accept the thesis that a focus on the beloved's beauty does characterize sexual love. Certainly as ordinarily used the term 'beauty' is too narrow, and arguably too sexist, to cover the kinds of pleasingness to the senses that are involved. I am sure, even then, that beauty cannot entirely explain the importance we attach to love. To start with, we find a value in love that we find in other relationships, for example with friends or family, whose beauty is not a factor (although the beauty of babies should not be overlooked). And again we surely find value not only in receptivity, in the contemplation of the beloved's beauty, but also in activity, in helping and giving. It is hard to think of this, as Plato seems to, as aimed at increasing the beauty we find. But the account may go further than we think, particularly in bringing out what is *distinctive* of love. Plato, we may recall, instances the possession of the beautiful as possession of the good. Later in Socrates' speech he remarks ((S), 210) that the lover 'will consider that the beauty of the mind is more honourable than the beauty of the outward form. So that if a virtuous soul have but a little comeliness, he will be content to love and tend him.' Qualities of character, we may agree, are more worthwhile objects of admiration for a lover than physical attractions. Yet we should not exaggerate this contrast. The aesthetic properties of a thing are, in the main, *expressive* properties. Beauty can be serene or tranquil – and these are qualities of character too, that can come out in the appearance.

This suggests that what we find physically lovable in the loved one is what is expressive of her admirable qualities, and what thereby provides a means of appreciating them; her smile expresses good humour, for example, her touch gentleness. Not every one that has such qualities can express them like this to everyone. Other people's good qualities may excite unappreciative reactions; their reliability may seem boring, their conscientiousness off-putting. And this is part of the reason why only the lover may be able to discern the beloved's finer features, and perceive them as attractive.

4.2   *Varieties of Love*

Plato on lovers

For Plato, in the *Symposium*, the value of love lies in possession of the good. But what does this *possession* of the good consist in? Since, as we have seen, one form of the desire for what is good, specifically for what is beautiful, is sexual desire, then sexual possession will exemplify possession of the good. Yet here, and in his other dialogue on love, the *Phaedrus*, Plato hedges this apparently natural conclusion around with health warnings. In the first place, sexual desire is thought of as essentially procreative. The point of heterosexual desire is begetting children, 'because to the mortal, generation is a sort of eternity and immortality ... and if ... love is of the everlasting possession of the good, all men will necessarily desire immortality together with good' ((S), 206–7). Plato sees that while sexual desire may be thought of as a desire for beauty, still some explanation is required of why it is an *appropriate* reaction to someone's beauty. His answer seems to be that the satisfaction of sexual desire tends to perpetuate what is beautiful through reproduction. Although this might count as an explanation of what the lover's desire to possess the good consists in, it seems wildly implausible as an account of sexual desire, not least because it makes the immediate goal of sexual desire merely a means to a further end.

In the second place, Plato warns against sexual desire itself as a dangerously uncontrolled reaction to beauty. In Socrates' first speech in the *Phaedrus* he says that

> the irrational desire which overcomes the tendency of opinion towards right, and is led away to the enjoyment of beauty, and especially of personal beauty, by the desires which are her kindred – that desire, I say, the conquerer and leader of the rest, strengthened from having this very power, is called the power of love. ((P), 238)

While in his second speech Socrates retracts this description as true of all love, yet it remains apt to describe that which is dominated by sexual desire. Since he is here describing homosexual love the *Symposium's* justification of sexual desire as an appropriate reaction to beauty is unavailable. Indeed it is seen as an inappropriate one, for, although it is a response to beauty, it is not, in the circumstances, a rational response. Rather, Socrates suggests that viewing the beloved's beauty as 'the expression of divine beauty' ((P), 251) will be the concomitant of a rational response, though what this amounts to is unclear.

Before we look further at the question how the value of sexual love might lie in the possession of the good we need to glance at two topics that inevitably engage our interest in Plato's theory: the position of so-called Platonic love (love without sexual activity) and the moral complexion of homosexual love. In Plato these topics are treated together, since Plato thinks both that homosexual love is potentially more valuable than heterosexual love, and that, despite this, it should be denied sexual fulfilment. Recent reactions to 'permissiveness' which canvass admiration of celibacy and opposition to homo-eroticism may incline us to treat them separately (see Scruton, pp. 34–43, 305–11).

First, Platonic love, which Plato sees as springing from the same sources as are manifest, in a limited and unreflective form, in ordinary sexual desire, and which Freudians, conversely, view as an aim-inhibited version of it. Both share, however, an assumption of common impulses, and debate as to how these should best be 'channelled': is sexual licence or sexual suppression the greater threat? But the 'hydraulic' model implied here has little to recommend it. On the one hand there are relationships that involve sexual attraction but stop short of intercourse. These will seem remarkable only to those with too narrow a view of the aims and satisfactions of sexuality. In particular cases they may be compared with more fully sexual relationships but there can scarcely be reason for a *general* preference. On the other hand there are those relationships that, even if they start from sexual interest, continue from a different, and, in particular, an intellectual admiration. But it is hard to see what the basis for a comparison, let alone a preference, between this kind of Platonic relationship and a sexual one would be. It is as if one were to compare parental love in general with deep friendship. And it would be a similar comparison too in that this non-sexual species of Platonic love seems more like a form of friendship than a kind of love.

Turning to homosexuality we see again, this time among its critics, a limited conception of the aims of sexuality. Particularly questionable is the stereotyping of sexual roles, identified without good evidence in heterosexual practice and carried over to homosexual activity in a way that leaves its participants looking ill-adapted as sexual partners. Plato's emphasis on beauty as the object of sexual desire has a tendency to counteract such simplification in two ways. First, it brings to prominence the possible variety both of what is found sexually beautiful and of what sexual responses register that beauty. Second, it permits, though in Plato's own exposition imperfectly, a symmetry in the relationship between sexual partners which allows their sexual desires to be the same in kind, not essentially distinct in virtue of their different roles. Yet Plato does leave room for the critique of those desires – more room, it may be felt, than is warranted by their exigency. He does so in a way that relates their aims and the activities required to pursue them to what we can see to be worthwhile in life. By what desires *should* we permit ourselves to be directed in the way we live our lives? If homosexual love were to be the subject of moral criticism it would need to be against a background of this kind of scrutiny. It is far from obvious what arguments might then be adduced to support such criticism. If homosexual love did differ from heterosexual love in point of its value this would have to be due to a difference in its place in lover's lives, not to some supposed metaphysical difference which does not show up there.

We may see from this digression that no straightforward evaluative comparison between Platonic and sensual love, or between homosexual and heterosexual love, is possible. The value of love is not something of which we can easily form a conception by fastening on one kind of love relationship and seeing how it is better or worse than others. But it would be wrong to think that Plato himself is offering quite such a comparison. Instead, he offers a comparison between loves that are, of their kind, more or less successful in fulfilling their reflectively revealed aims. Thus he compares procreative and sterile love, and, in particular, Platonic homosexual love with love's sensual forms. In this comparison Plato is addressing the question how love can have value through constituting possession of the good. It is the production of offspring which apparently provides an example of this, though it is, as I mentioned, an unsatisfactory one, since it makes love an *inessential* means to this commendable goal. A rational prospective parent might seek out a suitable mate for the production of genetically well-engineered progeny without a trace of passion, and many do. The only difficulty Plato could raise against this objection is that a beautiful mate is required for worthy offspring and that the passion of love is required for the recognition of beauty. Yet for the kind of beauty that one might reasonably intend to reproduce, the kind that is inter-personally recognizable, this condition would not seem to need to be fulfilled. We have to look elsewhere to find some good *only* achievable through love.

Plato seeks this in his ideal of Platonic homosexual love. This kind of love is, he insists, itself a kind of procreation by those 'who are more creative in their souls than in their bodies' ((S), 209). Such a person seeks 'a fair and noble and well-nurtured soul'; 'he tries to educate him; and ... brings forth that which he had conceived long before, and in company with him tends that which he brings forth; and they are married by a far nearer tie and have a closer friendship than those who beget mortal children'. The value of love is located in the possession of 'wisdom and virtue' achieved by the process of mutual discovery that is here described. Many features of the account seem unattractive, in particular, the emphasis on apparently rather narrow intellectual accomplishments and the presumption of an asymmetric educative process. Yet, if we disregard these, we can still see, I suggest, what Plato finds worthwhile in this kind of relationship. It is precisely that it is an *achievement*, something brought about by the successful application of standards, and hence possession of whatever good it is that those standards measure.

Plato's derivation of the relationship's value from its creativeness makes clear that it is an achievement that is valuable. It is its being a procreative relationship that makes it worthwhile. Procreation of the ordinary sort normally requires only a minmum adherence to 'standards'. Intellectual procreation is another matter; and we can see in Plato's assimilation of this kind of relationship to education the desire to find a way in which it must be answerable to more demanding requirements. Education is also, of course, a necessarily mutual achievement – a success for pupil and teacher both. And so, to be worthwhile, this kind of relationship must be educative. Perhaps 'wisdom and virtue' are not to be attained without such a relationship, though Plato suggests some seemingly supernatural routes to them. If so, education would be a fitting model for love, if we wish it to be the possession of some good not otherwise attainable. For love can then be seen as a relationship which it is rational to enter, and, in particular, as a rational response to what the beloved offers us. For there is, perhaps, a more *personal* kind of wisdom and virtue which is to be gained from it. What, though, is there to be said in favour of this kind of account?

Kierkegaard on romance

We need to see the account, as indeed Plato presents it, as a reaction to a view of love as irrational and unregulated and to a negative assessment of the value of such love. The nineteenth-century precursor of existentialism, Søren Kierkegaard, presents a similar opposition between what he terms 'romantic' and 'conjugal' love. 'I will indicate', he says,

> the mark by which romantic love may be known. One might say in one word that it is *immediate*: to see her was to love her ... Romantic love shows that it is immediate by the fact that it follows a natural necessity. It is based upon beauty, in part upon sensuous beauty ... In spite of the fact that this love is essentially based upon the sensuous, it is ennobled by reason of the consciousness of eternity which it embodies; for what distinguishes all love from lust is the fact that it bears an impress of eternity. The lovers are sincerely convinced that their relationship is in itself a complete whole which never can be altered. But ... since this assurance has undergone no test, has found no higher attestation, it shows itself to be an illusion. (Kierkegaard, (E), p. 823)

Lovers in this kind of relationship, then, are afraid of change in it, as well they might be, for 'even if it does not change, it still retains the possibility of change, for it depends on good fortune. But if what is true of fortune is true about happiness ... "call no man happy as long as he is living"; as long as he is living his fortune may change' (Kierkegaard,

(W), p. 295). Such happiness cannot be the possession of the good of which Plato speaks, for as the pleasures of love come so too, incomprehensibly, they may disappear.

Kierkegaard here catches a conception of romantic love with its attendant anxieties more accurately than Plato, since he does not confuse it with the onset of 'mere' desire. Yet it shares with mere desire the fact that it assails us in a way that elicits a response for which we can find no evident reason. That we continue to demonstrate this response therefore appears purely fortuitous. This is why we have no secure hold on the satisfactions of immediate love: we can find no reason why this object should continue to satisfy our desires in the way required to justify the importance we attach to it. The mutually responsive activities of immediate love are unregulated by the standards of an activity deliberately engaged in for a worthwhile goal. Such a love, Kirkegaard is suggesting, lacks the value that a relationship that was guided by such standards would have since its participants' responses are not offered as the *right* responses, as against the responses that it feels natural to make. But since they are not offered as the right responses, nothing stands in the way of their no longer coming naturally, or of their coming to seem the *wrong* response.

Beneath Kierkegaard's rather tiresome moralizing his doubts about the value of romantic love and his diagnosis of those doubts are surely persuasive. His recommendation of 'conjugal' love as a *duty* is less appealing. This notion imparts the standards required for love to be an achievement, and it does this without making love an inessential means to an end, as Plato's account threatens to do. But it not only leaves it unclear what good comes from the performance of the duty, it seems to make love dependent upon the strength of one's will rather than on one's capacity for spontaneously demonstrating the right response. In this respect Kierkegaard's conjugal love seems to lack a necessary feature of Plato's ideal relationship. Whereas Plato's lovers need 'self-control' ((P), 256) to achieve possession of the good through mutual development, what inspires them is a kind of 'madness' ((P), 251), an irresistible desire for what is good; so that the contrast is not between the spontaneous and the deliberate, but between spontaneously right responses and those spontaneous responses whose rightness, if they chance to be right, is no part of their explanation. Such an account, as we have seen, seeks to elucidate why we should love those whom we do. Kierkegaard's emphasis on the role of duty in a right relationship leaves this, like the value of such relationships in general, quite unexplained.

Here we seem to confront a paradox. If the value of love lies in an achievement then it seems to require regulation by the will. Yet regula-

tion by the will seems to be incompatible with the spontaneity required
for genuine love. For although 'love' can denominate a relationship –
and it is in this sense that we have been concerned with love – here it
also denotes a feeling, and the relationship is characterized by the
centrality of this feeling. How, we may ask, can a feeling be com-
manded? Yet if it cannot it is hard to see that whatever value we may
attribute to love it can be an *ethical* value.

4.3   *The Ethics of Friendship*

Aristotle on friends

On the type of view we are investigating, the value of love lies in the
fact that what the lover wants is worthwhile, so that the activity which
stems from the desire is guided by a sense of the worth of its object, and
what is gained by it is therefore achieved through adherence to standards by the lover. It is only because he or she has acted *well*, that his or
her love has value. And this, as I say, gives us a problem, for one acts
well only if one's acts are subject to one's will, while one's feelings seem
to lie outside of its control.

It is not in love alone that the proper exercise of the will in relationships presents a problem; though it is here that the problem is at its
most acute. We fall in love and, it is to be feared, we may fall out of love
again: how might the will be exercised in determining whether we shall
succumb to love or resist its dissolution? The problem arises for
friendship too: how might the will be involved in finding and keeping
friends? Indeed, perhaps there is but one kind of case here, for love is,
on some accounts, essentially a form of friendship: its value is the kind
of value friendship has. What that value is will depend on whether we
have chosen aright and remain true to each other. It is to Plato's pupil,
Aristotle, that we turn for the classic account of friendship.

Aristotle has no doubts that friendship is essential to the good life.
'No one', he says, 'would choose a friendless existence on condition of
having all the other good things in the world' ((E), bk 8, ch. 1). His
seventeenth-century follower, Lord Shaftesbury, gives the deficiency of
a friendless life an ethical aspect.

> Shou'd a Historian or Traveller describe to us a certain Creature of a more
> solitary Disposition than ever was yet heard of; one who had neither Mate
> nor Fellow of any kind; nothing of his own Likeness, towards which he
> stood well-affected or inclined: nor anything without, nor beyond him-
> self, for which he had the least Passion or Concern: we might be apt to

say, perhaps without much hesitation, 'That this was doubtless a very melancholy Creature and that in this unsociable and sullen State he was like to have a very disconsolate kind of Life'. But if we were assured that notwithstanding all Appearances the Creature enjoyed himself extremely, had a great relish of Life, and was in nothing wanting to his own Good ... we shou'd hardly, after all, be inclined to say of him 'That he was *a good Creature*'. (Shaftesbury, pp. 4–5)

How, we may ask, can it be that a creature with 'nothing wanting to his own Good' should be thought deficient? Shaftesbury's answer is that it is an inclination towards the good of one's own kind, not one's individual good, that determines whether one is a good Creature'. An inclination towards sociableness or friendship is necessary for that. Shaftesbury has a conception of what constitutes the good life for one's own kind in mind here, as the basis for his judgement on what inclinations are necessary. But is he not going round in a circle? Is not what constitutes the good life for one's own kind simply what is satisfying to its individual members, so that the value of friendship derives from the satisfaction it provides?

If that were so, then an easy answer to the problem of the role of the will in our relationships would present itself: we choose and maintain friends for mutual satisfaction, according to the principles of equity theory and the like discussed in the preceding chapters. Psychologists and sociologists commonly explain the existence of friendships and other social bonds as entered into from such motives. The Ik of East Africa, reduced to destitution when their hunting grounds were turned into a national park, come close to Shaftesbury's 'melancholy creature' in lacking close ties of affection. Their social order was brought to almost total collapse as a result of their terrible condition. Yet an anthropologist writing about the Ik tells us that 'the one bond that stood up was the bond of individual friendship ... a sort of bedrock below which even the Ik could not sink' (Turnbull, p. 150). The explanation for such bonds is, he claims, that they are 'formed for obvious reasons of economic gain' and 'observed only as long as observance is compelled' (ibid., pp. 201–2). We may well wonder whether if these are their motives the relationships described are really *friendships* at all. Is this kind of exercise of the will compatible with that description?

The imputation of such doubtful motives is, however, not clearly justified by the evidence presented. We can see the slide involved operating when a psychologist suggests that we may

explain altruistic behaviour by assuming that we value people and do things for them to the extent that they are in some way positively

rewarding for us .... This approach is well illustrated by the study of
friendship .... A friendship is viable when each party derives profit from
it .... It may seem that altruistic behaviour is somehow debased and not
truly altruistic when it is treated as part of the currency of a kind of social
bartering. (Wright, pp. 131–2)

These last doubts about the 'truly altruistic' character of friendship
depend upon the assumption that it is engaged in with the purpose of
obtaining mutual benefit. Yet this assumption is unjustified by the
evidence that only a mutually beneficial friendship is viable. Even if this
were true – and whatever may be the case with the Ik there are reasons
to doubt it as a generalization – still it would not follow that it was for
reasons of mutual benefit that friendship was engaged in. Yet only if it
was would friendly behaviour threaten to be 'not truly altruistic'; for
only then would friends have engaged in friendly behaviour for what
they could get out of it, rather than have engaged in behaviour which
happens to benefit them. 'Don't marry for money', enjoins the old
adage, 'but marry where money is.'

Aristotle has no doubt that many so-called friendships are formed
precisely for mutual benefit, but he regards them as 'inferior' friendships. Aristotle observes that 'it is between the elderly that friendships
of the utilitarian sort appear to be most frequently formed, the reason
being that in old age people are more disposed to seek profit than
pleasure .... But when it is young people who form a friendship the
object of it, we think, is the pleasure they get from it' ((E), bk 8,
ch. 3). It is not only of ancient Athenian society that this holds true,
though for the impoverished Ik, it seems, 'utilitarian' friendships are the
norm for young and old alike. The distinction here between pleasure
and profit is, however, not important to our present topic, since it is not
the pleasure of friendship *as such* which is in question. Both pleasure
and profit are here viewed as benefits for individuals which friendship is
instrumental in procuring, so that the value of these friendships lies in
their success in producing benefits and the rational exercise of the will is
in the pursuit of them.

Yet while Aristotle acknowledges that we 'must call those who
formed such connections "friends"', he insists that they are 'friendships
only by a sort of analogy or metaphor justified by the fact that there is a
kind of goodness in them, pleasure being a good thing in the eye of the
pleasure loving. And of course there is a sort of goodness in utility' ((E),
bk 8, ch. 4). The problem with calling these relationships 'friendships' is
that the partners' 'affection is not for the object of their affection as
such. These two forms of friendship then are grounded on an inessential

factor – an "accident" – because in them the friend is not loved for being what he is in himself but as the source, perhaps of some pleasure, perhaps of some advantage' ((E), bk 8, ch. 3). The appropriate motive for friendship is lacking: the will is exercised inappropriately in the choice of a friend and in the maintenance of the relationship. This seems correct. We do not choose *friends* for pleasure or advantage; rather we choose whom to *treat* as friends in this way (though when so treated they may become our friends). Aristotle makes much, too, of the way in which the inferior friendships end: 'sometimes when the lad's beauty wanes the friendship wanes also' or 'they part as soon as the profit goes' ((E), bk 8, ch. 4). If they were *really* friends, we would say, these would not be good reasons for breaking up: the fact that they do serve as reasons casts doubt on whether these are genuine friendships.

Good friends

The objection to choosing friends along these lines is just the one that we noted at the beginning of the chapter. The fact that they help us to pleasure or profit does not so far make them *worth* wanting, as friends. They might turn out to be quite undesirable characters. How then are we to choose whom to make our friends? It may seem as if *any* deliberate act of choice is incompatible with friendship (or with love). But this would be an exaggeration. One's sensibility to others, one's spontaneous feeling for them, is essentially involved in forming friendships. Yet sense, as in the title of Jane Austen's novel *Sense and Sensibility*, is counterposed to it; but how can it guide one's will?

In the book Marianne Dashwood, 'everything but prudent', with an 'excess of sensibility', falls for the 'uncommonly handsome' Willoughby, with his 'open affectionate manners'. 'Cold-hearted Elinor!' she chides her sister when all Elinor can say of her feelings for an admirer is 'that I greatly esteem, that I like him'. But Marianne is 'too frank' and she enters into a relation of intimacy with too little reserve. Even when Willoughby betrays her she still protests knowledge of his 'heart'. Her conduct was imprudent, but it was not so from failure to calculate what was in her interest, but from lack of *sense* in too hasty a judgement of the man. Cold-heartedness is indeed allied to insipidity, to lack of spirit, but also to selfishness. So Elinor's characteristic 'commendation' of Willoughby's rival, Colonel Brandon, is only 'comparatively cold and insipid', compared, that is, with Marianne's 'censure . . . prejudiced and unjust . . . so much on the strength of [her] own imagination'. Yet guarded as it is, Elinor's commendation is responsive not only to the 'attractions of Brandon's own good sense' but to him as, 'I believe, possessing an amiable heart'. Elinor does not lack sensibility but it is tempered by sense, and sense guides her choices.

Choice is quite properly exercised in questions of friendship, choice as to how reserved or open to be, how far to enter into friendly relations, in short whether to be friends. But this involves coldness or lack of feeling only if choices are made for reasons, as Aristotle would say, 'inessential' to the character of the friend 'in himself'. But what the man or woman is really like, not only how much I warm to them, *is* clearly relevant to whether to enter into friendship with them. Yet how is it? Aristotle's answer is that 'what is *absolutely* good and pleasant' – not just good for us or pleasing to us – 'is to the fullest extent worthy of our love and preference' ((E), bk 8, ch. 5). Elinor's 'esteem' and 'commendation' seem to reflect such judgements of moral worth. But do we, again, perhaps only have an extraneous factor? Surely a person's esteem for me may itself be, as Marianne suspects of Elinor's *cold*-hearted – not *responsive* to me in the way appropriate to friendship.

It may seem that esteem too is inessential to friendship. It may, like profit and pleasure, be necessary for the continuance of friendship, but, like them, not be a good reason for making friends. But this is surely a misleading comparison. It only happens to be true – at best – that friendship produces profit and pleasure: we can imagine it otherwise; but we cannot imagine true friendship without mutual esteem. We can be attracted to someone for whom we do not have a regard; but we cannot enter into friendship with him without coming to esteem him, blinding ourselves possibly to features of his character that militate against this. That was, in part, Marianne's failure of good sense: she acted from an opinion 'undiscerning', 'hastily formed', on account of her 'irresistible passion'. 'Liking', says Aristotle, 'has the character of an emotion, friendship of a confirmed disposition. Thus liking can be felt even for senseless objects: but that reciprocated liking which we call friendship involves deliberate choice' ((E), bk 8, ch. 5). The proper considerations in such a choice are whether I esteem a possible friend, and that requires me to reflect upon his character.

This brings me to a second difference between esteem and desire for profit and pleasure. It is easy to see how the latter can furnish a reason for acting, but how can the former? How can esteem be a reason for making friends, for surely, unlike those other desires, it *is* a good reason for my having the friends I do? The problem is that it cannot give me a *motive* for friendship, as I cannot choose to enter into friendship simply on the basis of esteeming someone – I have to like them first. It gives me a reason for friendship, I suggest, because to like them is already to be drawn towards friendship with them, and to esteem them is to judge that liking to be justified. I exercise choice in deciding whether to go where inclination leads.

Here, however, a falsely drawn boundary between the scope of the deliberate and the involuntary may well mislead us. It is not as if we were constantly having to resort to the stern exercise of the will to curb actions that would otherwise arise from involuntary inclinations. Our inclinations towards others are not directly under our control, but that does not mean that they remain unchanging and immune to critical scrutiny. Our inclinations are, of course, educable. We learn from the mistakes in our relationships, and are not so easily taken in by people who are only superficially attractive the second time around. Yet we can only learn like this by keeping our inclinations in check, so that, eventually, they no longer threaten to mislead us. Our desires themselves, then, can change in response to our readiness to permit them an expression.

To the extent to which we choose our friends, we exercise choice properly not in choosing what would satisfy us or even them, but in choosing what justifies our liking. The dating agency computer in operating on the former principle contributes no answer to the question how to choose friends well, only how to avoid dissatisfaction. Can it even do that? As Shaftesbury puts it, 'To love, and to be kind: to have social or natural Affection, Complacency and Good-Will is to feel immediate Satisfaction and genuine Content' (Shaftesbury, p. 61). Why cannot the computer encompass that? It cannot because friendly feeling is 'in itself original Joy, depending on no preceding Pain or uneasiness: and producing nothing but Satisfaction merely'. There are no desires or needs, in other words, with which we can programme the computer of which the joy of friendship is the satisfaction. 'A creature void of natural Affection and wholly destitute of a comunicative or social Principle ... feels a slender Joy in Life and finds little Satisfaction in the mere sensual Pleasures' (ibid., pp. 26–7). Yet if he had one desire less, his chance of satisfaction should be the greater. His 'misfortune and misery' lie in lacking something that makes life worthwhile: the assumption that this must be the satisfaction of our wants and needs fails to locate the satisfaction of friendship. This is itself *part* of the satisfaction of living well, and thus no factor instrumental to it. Like the satisfaction of getting anything right the dating agency computer cannot provide it, when it removes all risk of going wrong. The satisfaction of friendship is not, of course, self-satisfaction: it is one's friends with whom one is well satisfied. But this is a kind of satisfaction possible only if one can recognize one's good luck and avoid being blighted by one's bad.

This account captures, I think, one aspect of the way in which the value of friendship depends upon an achievement. It depends upon the achievement of choosing one's friends well, because one has chosen for what is really good in them. One has responded to their qualities aright, as one can do if one both has the right reactions and permits oneself to act on them only because they are right.

4.4 '*. . . love me for myself alone*'

This account of love and friendship may yet seem too *rationalistic* to be acceptable. It suggests that we should have reasons for loving or being friends with those who we love or befriend, so that the value of our relationships depends, in part, on whether we have good reasons. But talk of *reasons* here at all may seem out of place.

Love and friendship bind us closely to particular individuals and we set a special value on them precisely because of this. Yet it is hard to see how this could be justified if my reason for loving someone was their beauty or my reason for friendship with them their estimable qualities of character. For beauty or good character seem to give me a reason to adopt the same attitude to *anyone* who has them. But such widespread affections will not be a suitable basis for the *personal* relationships which we especially value. Aristotle puts this down to contingent factors: 'to have many friends is no more possible than to be in love with many at the same time' ((E) bk 8, ch. 6). The latter impossibility derives from the fact that 'sexual love involves an excess of emotion, such as can be naturally felt only towards one person', while the former is because, when you find a potential friend, 'you must become intimate with him and learn to know him before you make him your friend, and nothing is harder than that.' If we were *capable* of it, it would seem to be a good thing to have many more friends and lovers, since any suitable person would present me with the same reasons for a relationship.

Plato goes further and *commends* a widening of our affections as rational. Of the lover who finds beauty in a single beloved he says that

> soon he will of himself perceive that the beauty of one form is akin to the beauty of another; and then if beauty of form in general is his pursuit, how foolish would he be not to recognise that the beauty in every form is one and the same! and when he perceives this he will abate his violent love of the one, which he will despise and deem a small thing, and will become a lover of all beautiful forms. ((S), 210)

If this is not also the case with the love of 'virtuous souls' – and it seems unclear whether it is – that is only because the lover's interest is in 'fair and noble thoughts' in general, and these can be cultivated in *any* suitable soul, thus averting the need to extend one's circle of Platonic lovers (cp. Price, pp. 45–9).

Plato's picture of rational relationships is unappealing for a number of reasons. In particular, might not someone who was loved or befriended on Plato's principles justifiably complain that they were not loved for *themselves*, if they were loved for qualities that provide an equal reason for loving others? This complaint seems especially pertinent when it is a feature of his appearance for which the beloved is admired. For, as we noted in chapter 4.1, if an appreciative response to physical beauty is simply a generalizable aesthetic one it is insufficiently individual to be a basis for personal love. To complain that one is not loved for oneself is the complaint that one is not loved for what it is about one that makes a *personal* relationship with one possible (see chapter 6.1). Complaints that one is being treated as a 'sex object', for example, belong in this category.

We tend to think of one's character traits as contributing to what one is in a way that physical characteristics do not. But, if I love someone because of qualities of character that they have, again it seems that my attitude should be generalizable to others of similar character and will not therefore be appropriate to a properly personal relationship.

How are we to escape this difficulty? Can love and friendship really be offered on the basis of esteem without ceasing to be personal relationships? One suggestion would be that, since we need to *like* our lovers and friends, although we may *esteem* others we *cannot* admit them to our love or friendship because we do not sufficiently like them. But then that we love and befriend those that we do is explicable but not justifiable, since it is a mere happenstance that I like some of those that I esteem and not others. This is because, if liking and esteem are allowed to come apart, I cannot like people for the qualities that I esteem in them. Rather I like them for features that lack objective value while esteeming them for qualities that possess it.

This *divide* between sensibility and sense, passion and reason, is surely untenable. We do like people for many of the qualities that we esteem in them, kindness, gentleness and so forth. Yet we can like these qualities in some, while recognizing, though being unmoved by them, in others. We are able to *respond* to the kindness or gentleness of some but not of others, and that is what gives us a reason for love or friendship.

In fact, however, we think in terms of loving someone for *their* kindness or gentleness, not just for being kind or gentle. And this does not imply that their kindness or gentleness is of a special sort unique to them; only that it is an instance of a general sort displayed in a uniquely lovable way. Their kindness need not be idiosyncratic (as kindness to toads or television addicts might be); but their way of showing it must touch me with a particular poignancy. To love people for themselves is not, therefore, to be *contrasted* with loving them for their kindness or gentleness. But it does, I suggest, involve something other than founding our attitude merely upon a *judgement* that they are kind or gentle. For to judge that someone has an estimable character gives me no reason for adopting an attitude to them that I would not take up to anyone with similar traits.

This fact explains why it is, as we noticed in the previous section, that 'esteem' and 'commendation' can seem too 'cold-hearted' to be a basis for love or friendship. If these are merely *judgements* of moral worth then they are not appropriately responsive to the friend's qualities. An appropriate response does require liking them, and liking them first for what is really there, and second for what is worth liking. And this involves responding to something which cannot adequately be captured in judgements, whose truth *anyone* might accept without needing to have this response.

These two points about an appropriate response to friends or lovers are closely linked. For it may seem as if my choice must be guided by the twin questions: 'What is she really like?' and 'Is she, like that, worth liking?' But these questions can only be distinguished if I can describe her likeable features and go on to wonder if my response to such features is appropriate. Yet asking these sorts of question – even if it were possible – would seem an odd undertaking for a lover. The philosopher G. E. Moore (who influenced the Bloomsbury group of artists and writers through laying a special stress on the value of personal relationships) distinguished these questions as eliciting judgements of *fact* and judgements of *value* respectively (Moore, pp. 192–3). But the oddness and artificiality of asking them in relation to love comes over strikingly in an account of the sort of discussions common in the Bloomsbury set

> If A was in love with B under a misapprehension as to B's qualities was this better or worse than A's not being in love at all? If A was in love with B because A's spectacles were not strong enough to see B's complexion, does this altogether, or partly, destroy the value of A's state of mind? How did we know what states of mind were good? ... who was right when there was a difference of opinion? It might be that the two parties were not really talking about the same thing ... or it might be that some people had an acuter sense of judgement just as some people can judge a vintage port and others cannot. (Keynes, p. 87, p. 84)

The novelist D. H. Lawrence was quite appalled by it, saying of the Bloomsbury set, 'they want an outward system of nullity which they call peace and goodwill, so that in their own souls they can be independent little gods, referred nowhere and to nothing' (Lawrence, p. 247). 'Referred to nothing', because nothing *particular* could be the object of personal affection so construed. Good friends would be as interchangeable as good colleagues are supposed to be, since I only need to make the right judgements about their qualifications and about the merits of their possessing them.

Loving or befriending people for themselves, however, involves a response which is elicited by some feature of them precisely *because* it is a good feature to have. What is estimable in a person's character is commonly *likeable*, so that responding to another by liking them is a *single* response to a feature that they have which is worth liking, rather than a *pair* of responses, first of discerning some feature, and second of finding it estimable. Of course we can *think* we like someone through being in error either as to whether they have some feature or as to whether it is, in fact, estimable. (Two species of infatuation are possible in these cases.) But when we like someone for themselves, such an error is ruled out. That we avoid these errors in love and friendship is not just an accident, so that we do not *call* our attitude 'love' if it involves such an error. Rather, to be love our attitude must involve a responsive affection which is suitably discriminating towards the beloved's good features. In *his* case we must be reliable about them, although, of course, we may be far from reliable in responding to people's good qualities generally.

It is, as I have hinted, a brute fact about us that we respond differently to otherwise similar people. We like some and do not like others. Thus the ways their similar qualities are displayed strike us as distinctive and particular. It is at this level, which lies below that at which qualities can be easily classified and made the subject of judgements, that we discern what is specially likeable in them, or otherwise. Yet, as with the beauty of the beloved, the qualities of a friend may still be objective though concealed to the unfriendly eye. The fact that an emotional response is needed to discern them does nothing to show that these qualities are, like the hostility I detect in a landscape that frightens me, only a projection of my own response.

One very worthwhile thing about personal relationships, then, is that they give us access to what is good in other people in a way that reflects something good in ourselves, namely our capacity to recognize and respond to what is good. We have a particular admiration for those people who are able to love others whose good qualities are far from obvious, and we think of the love they bear them as particularly precious. And we feel a special revulsion at those who are so unresponsive to the qualities of others that they cannot form warm relationships with them. But such people are unfortunate too, since they are in large measure cut off from another benefit of love: the opportunity to have their own good qualities recognized and cherished within a close relationship.

Yet this brings us to a more general point concerning the limitations of the *kind* of account of love and friendship which Plato, Aristotle and many subsequent philosophers have offered. It is, as I have indicated, a kind of account that makes the value of love and friendship derivative from the value – by way of beauty or goodness – of the beloved or friend. Now this sits uneasily with the point just noted, that we have a particularly high regard for relationships in which one partner finds something lovable in the other, who is, overall, far from good. The account would seem to imply that the better the beloved or friend the greater the value of the relationship. Or perhaps rather, the greater the value of the relationship to the partner who has that beloved or friend. But it does not seem that our estimate of the value of a relationship, how splendid a love, how good a friendship, depends upon our view of the worth of its participants. And nor do we naturally think of its value as necessarily relativized to its participants, so that the *less* worthy partner derives the *greater* value from it. Rather we distinguish what each gets out of the relationship from the value that it has, so that one partner may get less out of it than the other precisely through failing to appreciate its value.

It is this sort of value on which Plato's and Aristotle's accounts throw little light since both see its value in terms of the benefits of well-directed mutual appreciation. Thus when love or friendship do not confer such benefits they are regarded as lacking value. Aristotle, for example, comments that 'the friendship of the unworthy is evil ... but the friendship of the good is good', ((E), bk 9, ch. 12). Yet this must leave something out of account since, though of course we have reservations about 'the friendship of the unworthy', still we regard their friendship as a saving grace in them. The reason is that although they have chosen badly, nonetheless they have achieved something worthwhile in maintaining and developing their relationship according to certain standards. Though Plato, in particular, recognizes that a worthwhile relationship requires such an achievement, this is, for him, because that is what accomplishes mutual appreciation. Yet it is hard to see why the value of an achieved relationship should depend solely on appreciation, rather than upon tolerance, trust, understanding or concern. More fundamentally, it is not clear why a relationship centred upon appreciation should generate *mutuality* at all. But it is surely the achievement of *mutual* understanding and the like which we particularly value in personal relationships. The value each partner has for the other is not separable from that.

Further reading

Plato's *Symposium* and *Phaedrus* are the astonishing seeds of all our thought on love and friendship. Antony Price's *Love and Friendship in Plato and Aristotle* is the most comprehensive guide to Plato's and to Aristotle's thought, G. Santas's *Plato and Freud: Two Theories of Love* is also worthwhile. Both authors explore this comparison. But what, if anything, in Plato's theory is still of interest today? Or is the world he writes about just too culturally remote? (See chapter 8.3.)

Kierkegaard's account of love is presented in *Either/Or*, especially volume 2 which is in the form of a 'letter to a young friend' by 'Judge Williams'. A dialogue on the nature of love between this imaginary character and the somewhat less imaginary Socrates of Plato's two dialogues would be interesting.

The eighth and ninth books of Aristotle's *Nicomachean Ethics* treat of friendship within the broad context of the good life. Is love a form of friendship? If so, is sex just an added extra? See Scruton's *Sexual Desire*, ch. 8.

5

Close Encounters

5.1 *Knowing Looks*

Sceptical doubts

'You won't finish that stocking tonight,' he said, pointing to her stocking, [which she was knitting] . . . .

'No,' she said, flattening the stocking out upon her knee, 'I shan't finish it.'

And what then? for she felt that he was still looking at her, but that his look had changed. He wanted something – wanted the thing she always found it so difficult to give him, wanted her to tell him that she loved him. And that, no, she could not do. He found talking so much easier than she did. He could say things – she never could. So naturally it was always he that said the things, and then for some reason he would mind this suddenly, and would reproach her. A heartless woman he called her; she never told him that she loved him. But it was not so – it was not so. It was only that she could never say what she felt. Was there no crumb on his coat? Nothing she could do for him? Getting up she stood at the window with the reddish brown stocking in her hands partly to turn away from him, partly because she did not mind looking now, with him watching, at the Lighthouse. For she knew that he had turned his head as she turned: he was watching her. She knew that he was thinking. You are more beautiful than ever. And she felt very beautiful. Will you not tell me just for once that you love me? He was thinking that, for he was roused, what with . . . their having quarrelled about going to the Lighthouse. But she could not do it, she could not say it. Then knowing that he was watching her, instead of saying anything she turned, holding her stocking, and looked at him. And as she looked at him she began to smile, for though she had not said a word, he knew, of course he knew, that she loved him. He could not deny it. And smiling she looked out of the window and said (thinking to herself. Nothing on earth can equal this happiness) – 'Yes, you were right. It's going to be wet tomorrow.' She had not said it, but he knew it. And she looked at him smiling. For she had triumphed again. (Woolf, pp. 113–14)

If there is one thing we most need to know, in getting to know someone, it is their feelings towards us. Mr Ramsey in Virginia Woolf's *To The Lighthouse* knows, we are told, that his wife loves him, although she will not say it. But Mr Ramsey is a philosopher and troubled with doubts. How does he know? How can he know that Mrs Ramsey loves him? We can discern in our ordinary doubts about other people's thoughts and feelings the seeds of philosophical scepticism, of philosophically grounded doubts about the extent of our knowledge. How could we know? Could we ever know the thoughts and feelings of others?

What, we may ask, has Mr Ramsey got to go on? Virginia Woolf mentions two bits of evidence as to her state of mind. First, 'it was not so' that she never told him she loved him. Though she did not do so in as many words she let him know by what she did for him. Her long-term behaviour is indicative of her love. But it does not, of course, indicate what she is currently feeling, at the point at which Mr Ramsey looks for a sign of love. So, second, 'instead of saying anything she turned ... and looked at him. And as she looked at him she bagan to smile, for though she had not said a word, he knew, of course he knew that she loved him.' Her movement, her look, her smile; these things express to him her current feelings of love. So identified, however, neither piece of evidence looks compelling. Someone could have many motives besides love – sexual love, for that is what is being talked of here – for taking good care of another. Kindness, pity or simply habit would be explanations; or again an ulterior motive involving a *pretence* of love might be suspected. Similarly a gesture, a look, a smile, even a word – the word for which Mr Ramsey is waiting – all these seem small things to base a judgement on. How easy it is to misinterpret them. How possible to be deceived.

We have here, then, the classic situation that prompts the philosophical sceptic to say: we do not know, we cannot know what another is thinking and feeling on the basis of *this* evidence, and yet there is no other. The sceptic's reason for doubt is that these behavioural tendencies or behavioural signs can be present even though the thoughts and feelings attributed on the basis of them are not present. But, he argues, if this is conceivable then no one who attributes thoughts and feelings on this basis can *know* that they are present. For someone else could be in as good a position as he was, could notice the behavioural tendencies and signs, but be too cautious to attribute those thoughts and feelings, and evidently he would not know. What is lacking, the sceptic insists, is a *proof* of the correctness of the attribution. But adducing evidence of the same sort cannot turn what we have into a proof, while no evidence of any other sort is available to us. Lacking proof, then, the sceptic says, we must lack knowledge.

So far the sceptical pattern of argument does not distinguish our claims to knowledge of other's minds from our knowledge of empirical truths in general. Exactly the same points could be made about our claim to knowledge of material objects. My sensory evidence always leaves open, it seems, the possibility of error from illusion, hallucination or dreaming: I might be deceived by Descartes' Evil Genius (*Meditation 1*) or his high-tech progeny, the mad scientist who keeps me stimulated as a mere brain in a vat (Putnam, ch. 1). In both these stories I have exactly the same sensations as I would if I were perceiving a world of material objects, and yet no objects corresponding to my sensations exist to be perceived. One who suspected such things and had no conclusive evidence against them would not lay claim to knowledge. Yet, says the sceptic, he who claims to know is in no better position and can therefore not sustain his claim.

But this general pattern of argument has little to recommend it, however hard it is to lay to rest. In the first place, the sceptic moves from alleging that something is conceivable to concluding that it is possible. Yet it is no objection to a claim to knowledge that what I claim to know might conceivably be otherwise; the only objection is that it is *possible* that it is otherwise. What we can conceive to be the case on the basis of our evidence may not in fact be possible. I can conceive or imagine that I am hallucinating, but in the circumstances I am in, neither suffering from a mental illness nor having eaten magic mushrooms or the like, it may not be possible that I am. In the second place, then, my evidence need not constitute a *proof* of what I claim to know. It must be such that it is not possible for what I claim to know to be otherwise, but it need not amount to a demonstration that it cannot be otherwise, for that would require that, given the evidence, I could not conceive of it being otherwise. Thirdly, while my evidence must make it impossible for me to be wrong it need not itself provide evidence of this impossibility. My evidence that I still have a blank sheet of paper before me must, in the circumstances, rule out the possibility of a depressive illusion, if I am to *know* that I have written nothing. But it will not, characteristically, be evidence that I am not under such an illusion. Rather it is *because* I am not that my sensory state does serve as evidence about the world. But it is because I lack evidence that I am not under an illusion that I can conceive of being under one. Fourthly, therefore, I can know something without having evidence that I know it; though the sceptic insists that the extent of my knowledge should be evident to me, in the way that knowledge gained by proof is evident. Yet in general to have conclusive evidence is one thing, and to have conclusive evidence that I have it is quite another. My doubts as to whether I know something will indeed lead me to doubt whether it is so. It does not follow that I need to resolve the former doubts in order to know, for, finally, the man who is not sure but is in the same evidential position as the man who is may, for all that, know what the latter knows.

Lovers' suspicions

All this may seem abstract and unconvincing until we apply it to examples like that of Mr Ramsey and his doubts. Before we do so we need to note again how very *general* the sceptical doubts can be. If I am to doubt whether someone loves me because I can't be sure that I know she does, should I not ask also if I can be sure that I *know* that her behaviour is what I take it to be, a look, a smile, and so forth, rather than a product of my imagination? And if I do not know this, can I be sure that I *know* that she has a mental life like mine at all? Soon these doubts become fantastical, as philosophical doubts are: they are not doubts which we can live with in sanity, unlike the ordinary doubts from which they issue. But if the ordinary doubts arise from arguments with the same form as sceptical doubts then there seems to be no principled reason why they should not be developed beyond the point where we can sanely entertain them. Something, then, needs to be said which might put to rest Mr Ramsey's doubts, were they themselves not neurotic, betraying, in a narrowly limited but emotionally charged area of his life, the *lack* of a rational assessment of the facts which is incipient insanity.

Mr Ramsey doubts that his wife's real feelings correspond to her behaviour. He knows she cares for him. He knows that she looks and smiles at him. But he doubts that she loves him. Only, it seems, words of love would satisfy him, though since the same pattern of doubt would still be possible we may well wonder if he would even then be reassured. But how might Mrs Ramsey's feelings fail to correspond to her behaviour? Perhaps her look and smile is deceptive. Perhaps she is pretending. Yet this hypothesis could be ruled out by further observations, as easily in principle as we can tell the difference between a real and a rubber egg upon our breakfast plate. And even if Mr Ramsey cannot, by reflection, thus satisfy himself that the smile is not pretence he may still know that it is not. That he cannot prove it does not show that he does not know. For, in the circumstances that Virginia Woolf describes, Mrs Ramsey does not look and smile deliberately, in the way that would be required for pretence. She does not do it to let him know she loves him, but she does it in a way that does let him know more surely than that would. For she looks and smiles spontaneously, as the feeling of love for him comes over her. Such a sign is, the novelist suggests, unmistakable to him: 'for though she had not said a word, he knew, of course he knew that she loved him.'

Mr Ramsey, we are to suppose, does know that his wife loves him, for he reads her looks and smiles correctly. He responds appropriately to them as looks of love. Then he is overcome with doubt as to the appropriateness of his response, since conceivably she is 'a heartless woman'. The reason for this is that although he can reliably judge what her looks betoken he does not know that he can. Yet that does not diminish his reliability. Like the nervous examination candidate, he may know even though he does not know that he knows. Like the examiner, Mrs Ramsey does know that he knows, for his responses to her looks are reliably correct.

We may wonder here how Mr Ramsey can get things right without risk of error when his evidence is insufficient to support a proof that he is right. In one way, perhaps, talk of evidence here may be misleading. Mr Ramsey has more to go on than he may be able to set out in a judgement as to his evidence. For the look and smile which are consistent with pretence or lack of heartfelt feeling may well be different from the look and smile which are not. Mr Ramsey may have no difficulty in telling the difference between a studied and a spontaneous expression, yet he may have no idea *how* he can tell the difference and hence no idea how to set down the distinctive character of a spontaneous expression in a statement of his evidence. He has a look to go on, but reference to that look indicates the general kind of sign he goes on rather than presenting any specific evidence that he has. Knowing the difference between a heartfelt and a heartless look, Mr Ramsey may, for all that, doubt that he knows, just because he does not know how he knows. How, though, *does* he know?

The most straightforward answer to this question is to say that Mr Ramsey knows his wife's look is a look of love because he knows her so well. The kind of reliability that is in question here is the kind that comes with long acquaintance and the sort of relationship that permits open and unguarded responses. To say he knows this because he knows her well is to explain the position he is in which makes the reliability displayed in his knowledge possible. It is rather as if one were to explain someone's confident judgement that a tiny chick is male by saying she knows because she is an experienced chicken sexer. This does not, of course, report her evidence or even the sub-evidential signs by which she tells. But it does explain why the judgement may be relied upon and can count as knowledge.

Many things that we know *about* people we know because, and only because, we know those people. To know them is not reducible, then, to knowing facts about them. It has a good deal more to do with knowing how to get on with them, with knowing how to respond appropriately and spontaneously to them. And yet it may still seem mysterious how we can do this, for, so far, none of the points in defence of the possibility of knowledge of others against sceptical doubts has specifically concerned the subject matter of that alleged knowledge, the fact that it concerns their thoughts and feelings. Yet this subject matter may seem to pose special difficulties for the potential knower, since, it may be said, the doubts about knowledge already considered concern only the outward face of things while thoughts and feelings lie behind the outward face. Is it not the case that with people, unlike other things (with the possible exception of animals), we can draw a distinction between facts that can be known through observation of what is outer and facts about what is inner which cannot? It is to this kind of scepticism, specific to our knowledge of other minds, and to the picture of the mind which it involves, that we must now turn.

5.2   *The Chambers of the Mind*

What gives rise to the picture of the mind as an *inner* place, not directly accessible to outward observation? It has its *philosophical* origins precisely in a contrast with the alleged uncertainties of all outward observation discussed in the last section. There, as we saw, I could always conceive of error with respect to conclusions based on sensory observation. Against this threat of universal scepticism the seventeenth-century philosopher René Descartes notoriously discovered a fact I could not conceive to be otherwise: 'suppose there were some extremely powerful and cunning deceiver fuelled with zeal to trick me. But there is no doubt that I exist in being deceived, and so, let him deceive me as much as he likes, he can never turn me into nothing as long as I think that I am something' (*Meditation 2*). What Descartes' argument, the so-called *cogito*, establishes, it seems, is that there is a range of facts about which I know without the possibility of doubt, namely facts that concern my mental functioning. It seems natural, then, to contrast these facts with those uncertainly grasped by outward observation as facts about what is *inner*. But natural as it seems, the picture it imports is highly questionable; for that there were some facts I could know indubitably would not imply that they were a different *kind* of fact, facts about different things, from any of the facts that I or others might grasp uncertainly. This, though, is what the picture of the mind as an *inner* place implies. It transmutes an apparent contrast between two ways in which some facts may be grasped – by outward observation or 'indubitably' – into a contrast between two kinds of fact — those that concern the outer and those that concern the inner.

Once we have the picture of the mind as an inner place the problem of coming to form reasonable beliefs about its contents on the basis of outward behaviour is inescapable. We can always conceive that the contents of someone's mind are other than as as we take them to be on this basis. No further evidence of the same sort can rule out such hypotheses. Yet such hypotheses can be known to be true or false in a way inaccessible to us, namely by the owner of the mind. Her ultimate reliability provides a standard to which we cannot aspire and against which our own judgements cannot be directly tested.

The picture is pernicious, since it invites us to think that we can *imagine* what the contents of her mind are in a way that does not view them as expressed in her behaviour, but which seeks to occupy her position in relation to them. Such fancies are only loosely connected with her behaviour. They spin around it – or, one should rather say, within it – a web of thoughts and feelings whose real existence we are powerless to determine. So they generate only anxiety, as in Mr Ramsey's case, or, in others, a kind of madness about the ascription of feelings in the context of behaviour which is, at best, opaque to such ascription.

Consider Mr Tebrick in David Garnett's *Lady into Fox*. His wife Sylvia, we are told, is suddenly turned into a fox! At first the fox continues to behave in a wifely way, even to the extent of playing a hand of cribbage, but soon her foxy nature begins to take over and lead her to attempt escape from him:

> ... his kissing and fondling her had very little effect now, for she did not answer him by licking or soft looks, but stayed huddled up and sullen, with her hair bristling on her neck and her ears laid back every time he touched her .... His wife's sullenness and bad temper continued that day, for she cowered away from him and hid under the sofa. (Garnett, (L), pp. 53–4)

Mr Tebrick's construal of the fox's behaviour in terms of the moods his wife might have had is something read into that behaviour from imagining her state of mind. But since it is a woman's state of mind that he imagines, and not that of a fox, his construal is meant to strike us as odd or even mad. Without such a construal he could not, of course, continue to love Sylvia, and so 'though we may think him a fool, almost a madman, we must, when we look closer, find much to respect in his extraordinary devotion' (ibid., p. 63).

It is, I suggest, only the picture of the mental as an inner place that can support such fanciful ascriptions of thought and feeling. In Mr Tebrick's case the fancy is forgivable! Elsewhere it is less so. Consider William Wordsworth, 'communing with nature':

> To every natural form, rock, fruit, or flower,
> Even the loose stones that cover the highway,
> I gave a moral life: I saw them feel,
> Or linked them to some feeling: the great mass
> Lay bedded in a quickening soul, and all
> That I beheld respired with inward meaning....
> Some called it madness – so indeed it was,
> If childlike fruitfulness in passing joy,
> If steady moods of thoughtfulness matured
> To inspiration, sort with such a name.
> (Wordsworth, 3, 127–32, 146–9)

Here the connections between the mental states ascribed and the outward signs observed break down almost completely. We have no need here to postulate mental states in explaining the changing 'face' of nature – weather and vegetation suffice for that – so that reference to its 'moods' are figurative, personifying not literal. Wordsworth's reactions, then, his eagerness to take such references literally, are to be explained by facts about him, not about the natural objects around him. Mountains became, it has been suggested by way of a diagnosis, substitutes for Wordsworth's father, who died when he was 14. His reactions towards his father were appropriate; transferred to mountains they are, at least incipiently, mad; just as Mr Tebrick's reactions, transferred from his human wife to a fox, are mad. Yet the picture of the mental as an inner place inaccessible to observation provides no firm ground for this distinction. For it gives no indication as to how what we conceive or imagine to be the case can go beyond what is possible.

The picture of the mental as inner does, however, derive from an important insight, even though it distorts and misapplies it. The insight is that to know about another's thoughts and feelings – about their current conscious mental state – we do have to be able to imagine what it is like to have those thoughts and feelings. We need, that is to say, to be able imaginatively to occupy their point of view as subjects of experience. The reason is, as Thomas Nagel puts it (Nagel, p. 436), that 'an organism has conscious mental states if and only if there is something it is like to *be* that organism – something it is like *for* the organism. We may call this the subjective character of experience.' Nagel goes on to identify the subjective as the *pour-soi*, the character that thought and action have as viewed from the point of view of their subject with her own experience of the world and what is desirable in it. The phrase '*pour-soi*' is Sartre's, and it is to his, and similar conceptions, that Nagel is alluding. In them, as we have already seen (chapter 3.4), the essence of a person lies in her point of view, to know about another person is to appreciate how things seem from her viewpoint.

Yet, as Nagel points out, this is precisely what we are quite unable to do in the case of organisms dissimilar from ourselves. We cannot, for example, imagine what it would be like to be a bat, with that creature's way of perceiving the world through hearing its to us inaudible high-pitched cries reflected off objects, quite unlike any of our own perceptual processes. We can observe the bat's behaviour and see how it relates to perceptual stimuli, needs and so forth. But none of this amounts to grasping its mental states. Nor will it suffice to add to this the imagining of *very* high-pitched echoes close at hand to which we can react *very* rapidly. This would simply to be try to imagine human mental states only loosely connected with the bat's behaviour. It is, however, precisely because we do not *behave* like the bat or *respond* to our environment as it does that we have no idea how to imagine its mental states. It is this fact which gives the lie to the Cartesian picture of the mind as an *inner* place. For what mental states we are capable of imagining depends upon what outward *behaviour* we can make intelligible to ourselves. What at bottom we imagine is what it would be like to find oneself *behaving* like this. But if this is so the mental is tied to behaviour in a way that the Cartesian picture makes impossible, for on that picture we can always imagine mental states quite disconsonant with the behaviour which we observe. We are not constrained, or at most very loosely, by the observed behaviour in our ascription of possible mental states.

The insight that to know about another's thoughts and feelings we have to be able to imagine what it is like to have them, and that, to do this, we have to be able to imagine finding ourselves behaving as they do, recovers our ordinary justifiable anxieties about knowing others from the general philosophical scepticism about this into which the Cartesian picture plunges us. For, of course, the minds of others can seem *impenetrable* and then the picture of the mind as an inner place can seem appropriate. In *To the Lighthouse* Lily finds Mrs Ramsey attractive but opaque.

> She imagined how in the chambers of the mind and heart of the woman who was, physically, touching her, were stood, like the treasures in the tombs of kings, tablets bearing sacred inscriptions, which if one could spell them out would teach one everything, but they would never be offered openly, never made public. What art was there, known to love or cunning, by which one pressed through into those secret chambers? ... could loving, as people called it, make her and Mrs Ramsey one? For it was not knowledge but unity that she desired, not inscriptions on tablets, nothing that could be written in any language known to men, but intimacy itself, which is knowledge. (Woolf, pp. 50–51)

It is however a grasp of what lies behind Mrs Ramsey's mysteriously assured behaviour that Lily is after here, not just knowledge of the words that go through her mind, the mental contents of which Mrs Ramsey might be reflectively conscious. That is why it is 'unity' that Lily desires, an imaginative sharing of what it is like to act with the tranquillity and understanding that Mrs Ramsey displays. How must she see the world to act like this?

One way of diagnosing the Cartesian error is, indeed, to see it as confusing the consciousness of the world with which people act, and which constitutes their range of current thoughts and feelings, with the reflective consciousness they have of these thoughts and feelings. Descartes is guilty of this confusion. Through taking the mind to be an inner place of which the owner has indubitable knowledge he equates consciousness with possession of this knowledge. But then what I am conscious of are facts about the inner mental world, the world of thoughts and feelings, rather than my thoughts and feelings being what constitute my consciousness of the ordinary outer world. Their essential connection with my actions in that world is thereby severed. Sartre's associate, Merleau-Ponty, puts the point well in his criticism of Descartes' *cogito*.

> It is not because I think I am that I am certain of my existence; on the contrary the certainty I enjoy concerning my thoughts stems from their genuine existence. My love, hatred and will are not certain as mere thoughts about loving, hating and willing; on the contrary the whole certainty of these thoughts is owed to that of the acts of love, hatred or will of which I am quite sure because I *performed* them. All inner perception is inadequate because I am not an object that can be perceived, because I make my reality and find myself only in the act. (Merleau-Ponty, pp. 382–3)

More needs to be said about the Cartesian picture of the mind, in particular about its account of a person's knowledge of their own mental states and the kind of privacy they have in respect of them. But first I want to explore further how in practice we acquire an understanding of those to whom we are close.

5.3   *Understanding People*

To understand another, I suggested, involves being able to see the world in which they act as they see it. But this is very schematic. What is it to do this successfully? Or what, to ask the same question in a way that may be easier to answer, is it to *fail* to understand them? If, as so often, one can succeed in only one way, failure can certainly take many forms. An extreme case of failure of understanding occurs between the young lovers Portia and Eddie in *The Death of the Heart* (Bowen, (D), p. 241) which we looked at earlier. Portia cannot understand how Eddie can love her but flirt with others. Eddie tries to explain:

> 'You know I love you: don't be silly. All I wanted was to be with you at the seaside, and here we are, and we are having a lovely time. Why spoil it for a thing that means nothing?'
> 'But it does mean something – it means something else.'
> 'You are the only person I'm ever serious with. I'm never serious with all those other people, that's why I simply do what they seem to want me to do. You do know I'm serious with you, don't you, Portia?' he said, coming up and staring into her eyes. In his own eyes, shutters flicked back exposing for half a second, right back in the dark the Eddie in there.
> Never till now, never since this half second, had Portia been the first to look away. . . .
> 'But you said', she said . . . 'that you need not mean what you say because I'm a little girl.'
> 'When I talk through my hat, of course I'm not serious.'
> 'You should not have talked about marriage through your hat.'

Portia's difficulty in understanding Eddie is to know if he is serious. But the difficulty is not just that he is commonly jocular. It is that even when he is not jocular his seriousness is in question. Eddie admits as much later:

> 'You expect every bloody thing to be either right or wrong, and be done with the whole of one's self. For all I know, you may be right. But it's simply intolerable. It makes me feel I'm simply going insane . . . you

apply the same hopeless judgements to simply everything ... for instance, because I said I loved you, you expect me to be as sweet to you as your mother.' (Bowen, (D), p. 339)

Eddie is unserious. His words and actions do not have the significance that comes from assured intentions. He does not act from settled principles and is, in consequence, unpredictable and feckless. Portia feels she does not know where she is with him. Not understanding him, she looks for significance in what he says and does. But she is baulked. The fact is that in Eddie's case there is no more to understand. What she sees is what she gets, as in that frightening glimpse of the real Eddie 'in the dark'. The image is precisely not one of hidden depths in Eddie's character, but of the lack of any lights by which Eddie is to be understood or to be guided by himself. For an image of depth of character can be applied only where there is seriousness, and where this is absent there is shallowness or superficiality. There is, in a sense, no interior to be penetrated here and so nothing to be concealed.

The notions of seriousness and consistency go together, so that we do, in a minimal way, *understand* a shallow person in grasping that he has no consistent reasons for action, no stable outlook on the world. But we could as well say there is nothing about him to understand. Certainly our understanding does not have the pay-off that understanding normally provides in terms of rendering the person understood relatively predictable and, if they are well disposed to us and so not motivated to defeat our predictions, reliable. Portia's lack of understanding is, for this reason, an extreme case. For the fault lies not in her but in the person whom she seeks to understand and it is a fault that makes any useful understanding, however much he invites it, impossible. There is no more for Eddie himself to understand than there is for Portia. I do not, of course, mean that Eddie has no character. Shallowness is itself a character trait and learning that a person has this trait tells us a good deal about them. It tells us, in particular, that they lack deep underlying feelings: Eddie, as we saw, is incapable of love. The reason is that feelings run deep to the degree to which they affect a person's whole life, providing wide-ranging reasons for action which shallow people lack.

Asking whether someone is serious or single-minded contrasts with asking if they are engaging in pretence or concealment. The latter requires the ascription of principles of action which are dissimulated or hidden, but which could be sincerely expressed or openly revealed. Pretence is, indeed, a form of concealment, though it involves an intention not only to conceal but to deceive. It is not, therefore, as the picture of the mind as an inner place makes it appear, simply a sort of screen which hides the real feelings. It is also, as an act of pretending (though not, of course, as the act which constitutes the pretence), an *expression* of thought and feeling; for if I learn that someone's acts are a pretence I normally come to know that their feelings towards me are cold and calculating, not warm and spontaneous. I know something of how they view me and, perhaps, people in general. While pretence is a form of insincerity mere concealment indicates only secretiveness or closeness (in the sense in which this contrasts with openness). Or rather this is what concealment indicates when it is undertaken deliberately, with the intention that another should not find out about one. But there are limits to deliberate concealment – it is hard to conceal the fact that one is engaging in it. So, when another learns that one is, they *do* find out about one: they find out that one is secretive or close, that one does not want others to know about one. And one can intend that others should find out that one wants them not to know: one can be *coy*.

Not all concealment of one's thoughts or feelings however is deliberate. Those who are merely shy or naturally reserved are not secretive or close (Mrs Ramsey in *To the Lighthouse* is evidently an example of such reserve or diffidence). They may find it hard to express their feelings so that it is difficult for others to understand them. But it is the *deliberate* expression of feeling that is hard for them. Shyness is not a kind of autism in which emotion – if it is felt – is not expressed. Shy people unguardedly express their feelings, as others do, but, becoming aware of these expressions, they are embarrassed and seek to check them. They cannot easily let other people be close to them (in the sense in which closeness contrasts, metaphorically, with distance). There is, and it is a most important fact, both deliberate and spontaneous expression (or the withholding of expression) of thought and feeling. Were there not the former there could not be close relationships in which people can *let* others come to know them intimately. Were there not the latter any knowledge of others would be difficult or impossible.

Spontaneity and deliberateness, however, are not contraries. We can commonly choose whether to express our thoughts and feelings, and in this sense, their expression is then deliberate. The expressive act, the weeping or the laughter, does not thereby become deliberate: it need not be studied laughter or insincere tears. But though these expressions of feeling may be spontaneous they are, commonly, within our control. So others may fail to understand us just because we exercise that control to prevent them. We do not want them to get to know us, and, with different degrees of effectiveness, we can frustrate their efforts to do so. We do not betray to them what it is we find desirable by a direct expression of our reactions to it. Since a close relationship is one in which the partners do not, except for special reasons which introduce difficulties into the relationship, conceal their feelings from each other, it follows that one reason for failing to understand others is failing to form a close relationship with them. And this can happen for many reasons. In particular I may fail to command their trust. I shall have more to say on this matter in 5.4.

A close relationship can also fail to develop despite the best efforts of the prospective partners because one of them does not pick up or attune to the spontaneous expression of feeling which the other vouchsafes to them. Consider Newman, the rich New World hero of Henry James's *The American*. His fiancée, the aristocratic French widow Madame de Cintré, breaks off their engagement:

'Why, why, why?' he cried. 'Give me a reason – a decent reason. You are not a child — you are not a minor, nor an idiot. You are not obliged to drop me because your mother told you to. Such a reason isn't worthy of you.'

'I know that; it's not worthy of me. But it's the only one I have to give. After all,' said Madame de Cintré, throwing out her hands, 'think me an idiot and forget me! that would be the simplest way.... I am timid and cold and selfish. I am afraid of being uncomfortable.'

'And you call marrying me uncomfortable!' said Newman staring....

'What are you going to do?' he asked, 'where are you going?'

'Where I shall give no more pain and suspect no more evil. I am going out of the world.'

'Out of the world?'

'I am going into a convent.'

'Into a convent ...'

'The idea struck Newman as too dark and horrible for belief, and made him feel as he would have done if she had told him that she was going to mutilate her beautiful face, or drink some potion that could make her mad. He clasped his hands and began to tremble visibly.

'Madame de Cintré, don't, don't!' he said. 'I beseech you! on my knees, if you like, I'll beseech you.'

She laid her hand upon his arm, with a tender, pitying, almost reassuring gesture. 'You don't understand,' she said. 'You have wrong ideas. It's nothing horrible. It's only peace and safety.' (James, pp. 247–52)

There is a terrible irony in her last remark, for what Newman had offered the sad Madame de Cintré in proposing marriage to her was safety: 'With me ... you will be as safe ... as safe,' he said, with a kind of simple solemnity, 'as in your father's arms' (ibid., p. 164). But it is just from the terrible pressure of her family that the convent does give safety.

The breakdown of the engagement is a metaphor for the lack of understanding between the betrothed. What Newman means by comfort and safety is something quite different from what Madame de Cintré means by these words. While each is deeply attracted by the other no closeness is possible. To Newman, independent and self-reliant, her sense of obligation to others and conformity to customary norms are unintelligible. He simple cannot imagine what it is in her that checks, and finally breaks, their relationship. And so he can only view it as idiocy or madness, as what is beyond a rational explanation. Much as she would wish him to understand there is nothing that Madame de Cintré can do to make him. The distance between his principles of action and her own is just too great; his simple conviction in the exclusive rationality of his own is too strong. It is this which make her very expressions of feeling opaque to him. Her words and gestures produce perplexity, not illumination, since he cannot respond to them with sympathy and understanding. He can, we may say, only observe and wonder, a tourist in a foreign land.

Contrast poor Newman and Madame de Cintré with the lovers Robert and Stella in Elizabeth Bowen's *The Heat of the Day*.

> His experiences and hers became harder and harder to tell apart; everything gathered behind them into a common memory – though singly each of them might, must, exist, decide, act; all things done alone came to be no more than simulacra of behaviour: they waited to live again till they were together, then took living up from where they had left it off. Then their doubled awareness, their interlocking feeling acted on, intensified what was round them – nothing they saw, knew or told one another remained trifling; everything came to be woven into the continuous narrative of love; which, just as much, kept gaining substance, shadow, consistency from the imperfectly known and the not said. For naturally they did not tell one another everything. Every love has a poetic relevance of its own; each love brings to light only what is to it relevant. Outside lies the junk-yard of what does not matter. (Bowen, (H), p. 94)

Mutual understanding here consists in the possibility of seeing the world in the same way, not in all respects, but in those that are 'relevant' to their love. But how, it may be asked, can a 'doubled awareness', actually understanding *things* in the same way, entail understanding one another?

This question arises from the mistaken assumption that knowing or understanding another consists in apprehending a special range of facts –

facts about the mind – rather than apprehending ordinary facts in a special way, namely the way in which another person apprehends them, with her distinctive desires and purposes. For the latter we have to share with those we understand a sense of what in the world it is possible to find desirable, even when our actual desires are not the same. Thus our understanding comes out in the appropriateness to their acts of our responses, which are responses to the world concordant with their way of viewing it. But responding appropriately does not just involve producing a pattern of responses which is appropriate to some true generalization about their behaviour – their not liking loud noises or hurried movements, for example. To respond thus would not so far be to understand them rather than to know how to treat them, in the way some people become skilled at treating the old or the very young. This is because it requires no *cognitive* grasp of their condition, no sense, for example, of how unnerving the world of noise and hurry seems. Skilful as we are at humouring them, we may be unable to respond to those who see the world like this.

What we grasp about those to whom we can respond is not easy to classify or conceptualize. When it is a feature which distinguishes a particular individual's outlook on life, the aspects of a person's principles of action that distinguishes them from others, then it is the kind of feature we spoke of earlier (in chapter 4.4) as what we appreciate in loving someone for themselves. Loving or liking someone as a friend, and understanding them, come close together here. For to love or feel friendship to them involves being able to respond to their distinctive features and wanting to do so because of the attractiveness of the outlook they embody. And this implies finding them transparent and unperplexing in a way that leads us beyond understanding their experience towards sharing it (though the sharing of experience, it should be noted, need not strike us as the experience of sharing, which in love it often does).

Emphasizing the sharing of principles of action may seem simply like a reiteration of the banal observation that 'like is attracted to like.' This is because, psychologists suggest (e.g. Duck, pp. 81–5), 'every similarity between us and a partner reduces uncertainty.' In developing a relationship we 'filter' our partner through increasingly subtle comparisons with ourselves 'because we wish to understand and create a thorough picture of the partner's mind and personality in as much detail as possible' in order further to reduce uncertainty. Yet what is suggested by a 'picture of the partner's mind' is indeed knowledge of a class of facts normally concealed from us. Further, there is an ulterior motive for acquiring such knowledge and restricting our circle of friends to those about whom we can acquire it, namely the desire to reduce uncertainty. What is described here is not, if taken literally, the kind of understanding that grows naturally in a close relationship. Developing relationships with those whose principles of action we can share over a range of issues is not something we do for a motive. It is, given the kind of understanding involved, all that we are *able* to do, and in doing it we are relieved, but not in a way we can contrive, of some of our uncertainties.

5.4   *Intimacy and Commitment*

> To be friends or lovers persons must be intimate to some degree with each other. Intimacy is the sharing of information about one's actions, beliefs or emotions which one does not share with all, and which one has the right not to share with anyone. By conferring this right, privacy creates the moral capital which we spend in friendship and love. (Fried, p. 142)

The *privacy* of thought and feeling, metaphysically mislocated by the Cartesian picture of the mind as necessarily private, directly accessible only to its owner, is in large measure restored to its proper place in this suggestion. Privacy safeguards us only against *unwanted* intrusions. It excludes strangers, but it is no barrier to friends. Indeed it is into our private lives that people step when they become our friends and lovers.

The privacy of thought and feeling presupposes control of their expression, which is granted to friends but not to strangers. Yet it is surely not 'information' about our thoughts and feelings which is shared with the former and denied to the latter. This implies the view, that knowing others is gaining *propositional* knowledge of facts about them. But when I want others to know me it is not propositions that I want them to acquire – though these may help. It is appropriate reactions. Worse than this implication, however, is the assumption that the way I reveal myself to others is through *having* information about myself which I can go on to reveal. This is too close to the Cartesian picture for comfort. For though I can sometimes say to another just what I think and feel, I commonly cannot. And then I may need a friend to *help* me to find out. Another can tell me from the way I express my feelings *what* these feelings are – give me propositional knowledge of them. Or it may not matter if they cannot, since at least I have given expression to them, and this expression has been understood.

What is shared with friends and lovers in intimacy is not information about my thoughts and feelings. It is, however, something I can, if I choose, keep private. What I share with intimates, or keep private, is rather my thoughts and feelings themselves. To share them is to express them to those able to understand them, with the intention that they be understood. But though sharing our thoughts and feelings requires this intention, it need not – and probably will not – be the primary intention that I have in expressing thoughts and feelings, to friends. Obviously I want them to know what I feel, but not necessarily because I want them thereby to find out about me. I may, more likely, want them to find out something about the world beyond me, by finding out what I feel about it. And this, of course, further undermines the idea that I want to share *information* about myself, for I here want someone else to see things as I do, not to see me as I see myself.

In an image of this sort of sharing, similar to that met earlier in *The Heat of the Day*, David Garnett describes the lovers in *A Shot in the Dark*:

> It was being two and not one: yet one, part of the time: the two seeing, tasting, touching, smelling the same things simultaneously; laughing and talking together; every external thing sparkling with new freshness because seen by two. That was love. Love to be pictured not by two figures in an interlocked embrace of mutual possession, but by two figures side by side: eager, darting forward, like dolphins leaping, leaping to turn the flying fish of ecstasy to one another. (Garnett, (S), p. 51)

What I want to take from this idea is its rejection of love as *mutual possession*, as in Sartre's despairing account (see above, 3.4) and the alternative it offers. Sartre claims that the lover wishes to possess the other's 'freedom', her principles of action, in a way that makes it possible for him to control her. But he also wants to possess it 'as freedom', so that she continues to act spontaneously, not because he manipulates her acts. And this is impossible. One thing this implies is that the lover wants to gain *knowledge* of the other of a sort that he can use to influence her behaviour in a way that suits his own ends. This need not come to exploiting her weaknesses, in the manner of a seducer. It may simply amount to deliberately tailoring his own behaviour to fit what he knows of its effects on hers. Either way the knowledge that is sought is not disinterested: it is acquired with a view to establishing possession. And that, we may object, is not to acquire knowledge of the beloved with the motives that a lover – or indeed a friend – should have.

Yet it is this model of our knowledge of others which informs the view of the role of privacy quoted at the start of this section. I share information about myself only with those I can trust not to use it in a way that is instrumental in achieving their own ends. I share it only with those I can trust to use it to further my own ends. In either case the knowledge the other gains would not be disinterested. It would be sought for a purpose, and the question I need to ask in deciding whether to grant it is whether the pursuit of that purpose would benefit me or not. Such knowledge would be propositional, since it is upon the truth of certain propositions about one that others will characteristically rely in planning actions to fulfil their purposes. On this view, when I trust others who are admitted to intimacy with me I trust them not to exploit or misuse the facts I give them knowledge of.

The alternative view sees intimacy quite differently. It sees it as arising from putting someone in a position where they are privy to spontaneous expressions of feeling that others are not, and who may be able in consequence to develop patterns of response appropriate to what I feel. Such patterns of response constitute a kind of knowledge of me that (whilst it can, of course, be compatible with two-timing or betrayal) cannot be *exploitative*. This follows from its being non-propositional and hence not adapted to a variety of purposes, some not friendly. The trust I bestow on you in intimacy is the trust that you will take up this attitude of responsive understanding. And this attitude militates against your taking up the stance of an unresponsive observer collecting propositional knowledge about me which could be misused. In this sense love is indeed blind.

I have highlighted these contrasting views of intimacy and of the kind of knowledge it gives access to in order to emphasize one difference between *personal* relationships and those that are relatively impersonal. It is, I suggest, relationships that provide the intimacy that requires a responsive understanding which we think of as personal. And again I have indicated how this kind of understanding involves appreciating people for themselves. The mere sharing of information about ourselves, however, does nothing to create personal relationships. We tell intimate things to our doctors, priests or strangers we meet in trains and know we will never see again. We do so in contexts in which personal relationships are out of the question. It would, I have implied, be quite wrong to regard personal relationships as differing only in degree from these, differing, that is to say, only in the amount of information I disclose (see also 6.1).

I have emphasized the role of trust in our control of the expression of our feelings which allows others to share them with us, to become intimate with us. The sincere acceptance of trust is commitment. I trust others with my feelings only if they would thereby be committed to an appropriate attitude towards them. They would not, other things being equal, scoff or sneer or take advantage of me. So one of the things I often need to know about others is whether they have this commitment. When someone asks, 'Do you love me?' it is commonly the existence of a commitment for which they seek confirmation.

Analogously when someone asks, 'Do I love him?', they are often wondering if they have the required commitment. How can anyone be in doubt about that? On the Cartesian picture we each have direct access to our minds and can easily discern the thoughts and feelings that pass through it. Perhaps we could not easily put them into words, but this does not seem to be the only kind of doubt we can, in practice, have about them. In Elizabeth Bowen's *The Hotel* Sydney, a young woman on holiday, agrees to marry a fellow hotel guest, Milton: 'I do want to,' she says, 'you know I do want to.' But later, after a near accident, she revises her view of the truth of this avowal.

> 'I am afraid,' she said, 'but it's quite impossible ... our marriage.'
> 'Oh!' he said quietly. 'Oh!' 'I don't know how we could ever have thought of it.'
> 'I am afraid' he said slowly, 'I can't see yet why it's not right'.
> She looked hopeless, 'I suppose I can't make you see. But I do know.'
> 'Since when?' She seemed protected by some kind of exultation, so he let out his pain in sarcasm. 'Recently Sydney?'
> 'Just now. I suppose it was the shock of being alive – oh, how can I explain it to you? I had no idea we were as real as this. I had never realised it mattered so much ... *Now* I understand – but it seems I ought to tell you what I didn't understand. I think we have been asleep here; you know in a dream how quickly and lightly shapes move, they have no weight, nothing offers them any resistance. They are governed by some funny law of convenience that seems to us perfectly rational, they clash together without any noise and come apart without injury ... we have taken nothing into account. You and me – how could we ever have thought of it? it was just a dream. It seemed simple.' (Bowen, (H), p. 159)

On the Cartesian picture, of course, one thing I can be certain of even in a dream are my thoughts and feelings. But here the impression of those feelings is itself judged to be misleading, dreamlike.

When Sydney asks herself whether she really wants to marry Milton she is not simply reflecting upon her state of mind. She is asking a question which calls, in part, for a decision. She needs to decide whether the reasons for marrying him really are, by her standards of what is desirable, good reasons. She cannot (as we noted in 2.5) rest content with the observation that she is disposed to act as if they were, since this would involve abnegating control of her own behaviour. She cannot take up an uninvolved observer standpoint towards her own mental states and see which way they lead her. She has to determine whether she should be led in that direction. Nor is this true only of her *current* mental state. She also needs to see whether her past mental state really sprang from her persisting standards of desirability, or whether her thought at the time that it did was an illusion. This is indeed what Sydney concludes. She takes herself to have been wrong in thinking she wanted to marry Milton, wrong because she did not at that time seriously ask herself if she did consider the reasons and decide upon them.

This example generalizes, I believe, to account for very many cases of our knowledge of our own mental states. Knowledge is often based upon decision. It is this which makes it possible for our knowledge of our attitudes to others to constitute commitments to them. Where our attitudes to them are of a sort to invite trust we can accept that trust by demonstrating commitment. What others want to know about us is whether we have made this commitment, whether we have reflected upon our attitudes and made a decision to act consistently in a way that can be relied upon. But that comes out as much in how we act as in what we avow to be our good intentions.

In this chapter we have applied and developed the general account of understanding human behaviour put forward in chapter 2 to the particular case of understanding the behaviour of those whom we know well. Here again, I have suggested, we need an account in terms of grasping people's reasons for acting, and to grasp them we have to see what it is to that they find desirable. This commonly comes out in their spontaneous reactions to circumstances, which express their thoughts and feelings. But we shall only understand these if we can to some degree imaginatively enter into those reactions and this requires some sharing of what we are both able to find desirable. Now why, we may ask, should we *want* to understand others in the way we understand those we know well?

An answer to this question must contribute, I suggest, to an account of the *value* of close relationships which we discussed in chapter 4. For if we value close relationships because they enable us to get to know people well then their value must surely derive, in part at least, from such knowledge. But such knowledge is, I have argued, disinterested, not acquired for further ends. It must then, like knowledge in general, be something we value for its own sake. Here, if I am right, we cannot explain this in terms of the superiority of knowledge to ignorance or of truth to error, for propositional knowledge is not involved. Yet my knowledge of another in a close relationship still constitutes an awareness of what they are really like, though my reliability about them comes out in my behaviour rather that in my judgements. It is simply better to get such things right about people in this way than to get them wrong. We cannot imagine ourselves not regarding it as especially desirable to do so.

Further reading

On knowledge and scepticism *An Introduction To Contemporary Epistemology* by Jonathan Dancy can be recommended, especially chapters 1, 2 and 5 (which contain an up-to-date treatment of the other minds problem). John Wisdom's *Other Minds* is still instructive and entertaining. People who know one another well are said to be able to read each other's minds. What account of this kind of knowledge might we give?

The Cartesian picture of the mind and criticism of it are the staple fare of contemporary philosophy of mind. I suggest Smith and Jones's *The Philosophy of Mind*, while Nagel's 'What is it like to be bat?' and related papers in his *Mortal Questions* should not be missed. How like ourselves do other creatures have to be to be intelligible? Are women, for example, intelligible to men and vice versa?

The proper limits of personal privacy have, of course, become a legal question. Charles Fried's *An Anatomy of Values*, especially chapters 5 and 9, and Jeffrey Reiman's 'Privacy, Intimacy and Personhood' are particularly suggestive. What rights to privacy should we have and why?

6

Freedom and Fraternity

6.1 *Private Affairs and Public Business*

Personal relations

Personal relationships like love and friendship are just one kind of social relationship. They require trust and commitment and they demand that each of these attitudes be reciprocated. But so do many other kinds of relationship. Colleagues, most often bound together by far less than love or friendship, have to trust one another, at least to some degree, to behave towards each other in accordance with professional standards. And that trust is based on a presumption of mutual commitment to these standards; a commitment, for example, to criticize one's work for its errors – not as a stratagem to impede publication – without which discussion among colleagues would be pointless. So in looking at the reciprocity involved in such relationships it is as well to take more general cases than the purely personal. But first it is worth asking what it is that distinguishes what we call *personal* relationships from other social relationships characterized by the same sort of reciprocity.

At least two kinds of answer suggest themselves. One distinguishes personal from other formally similar social relationships by the different sorts of objective of the activity that they involve; the other by the different characterizations of the parties who are related. Perhaps an adequate account requires mention of both. The first kind of answer might suggest that the point of personal relationships is the *overall* well-being of the parties involved. They are, we might say, relationships with the *whole* of a person. Friends, for example, are concerned for each other across a very wide range of matters which affect their welfare and happiness: they are concerned for them not just in their jobs but in their marriages, not just for their health but for their happiness. Colleagues, by contrast, need be concerned for each other only in matters related to their jobs and in whatever else bears on these; and then they need be concerned only for their intellectual health and not their happiness at work. Social relationships, then, contrast with personal ones as requiring mutual concern over a much more restricted range of matters affecting the parties' well-being.

There is some plausibility in this kind of answer. It does not fall foul of the objection that we do not *enter* friendship in order to promote mutual well-being, for, even if we enter it without such a motive, we still incur obligations to promote the well-being of our friends. We do, of course, have a general duty to act in a way that promotes anyone's well-being, rather than the reverse. But over and above this we have special obligations that entitle our friends or family to claim preferential treatment by comparison with 'just anyone'. While the justifiable extent of such special obligations is open to question (see 8.1), their existence cannot be doubted. Yet two difficulties with the account present themselves. First, it makes it hard to see how friendship, love and close family relations might *differ* in respect of the ways they aim at the well-being of those involved. And yet they seem to do so. While family membership imposes obligations to give aid in times of distress, for example, it does not, notoriously, require amiability; and while friendship requires amiability it does not license demands for assistance. Neither requires us to aim at *overall* well-being, although admittedly they do come close to it. Secondly, the account exaggerates the extent to which non-personal reciprocal social relations aim at *well-being* at all. Work-mates generally need to be able to rely on each other through the existence of trust and commitment, but it is the quality of the job which requires this, not their own well-being. The promotion of their skill and efficiency is, indeed, only a means to this end, and one not necessarily conducive to their well-being if, say, it leads to actual, or intellectual, myopia. The first kind of account is, then, defective, though the contrast it relies upon may well suggest an acceptable *necessary* condition for the distinction.

I turn, therefore to the second kind of answer to the question of what is distinctive of personal relationships. This suggests that these are relationships which relate persons as the particular individuals they are, rather than only as the occupants of social roles. It emphasizes the feature, investigated earlier, which marks out genuine love or friendship as that which relates us to a *particular* individual for their own sake. On this view Aristotle's friends for pleasure or for profit will be in the nature of playfellows or business partners rather than personal friends.

Their relationships will be merely social rather than personal, since it will be qua compatible pleasure-seeker or profit-maker, with whom I enter an association or with whom I find myself in one, that I am on friendly terms with them. Anyone in the same role could expect the same treatment. And it is this which characterizes non-personal reciprocal social relations (although it has to be said that in many such relationships we do come to value the particular individuals we are related to, so that there is no sharp dividing line between the personal and the social).

I believe that this account is largely correct, though no doubt in need of refinement. But it is worth considering the objection that it misclassifies *family* relationships as non-personal, on the grounds that *anyone* who was my son or daughter, say, not just the particular people who are, could expect the same treatment. One response is just to accept that family relations are, anyway, simply *as such* non-personal; that though they may *generate* personal relations they are in themselves non-personal since they do not necessarily involve intimacy or even affection, which measure the closeness of a relationship. Yet this would, I think, be a misunderstanding. So far in dealing with *close* relationships we have considered only close *personal* ones. But the concepts of the close and of the personal are in fact independent. Colleagues can be close and, indeed, enjoy intellectual intimacy and warm mutual regard. But this does not put their relationship on a personal level. It is, as the first kind of account of the personal suggests, too *limited*, and as a result is compatible with behaviour too unfriendly to be countenanced in a personal relationship, though commonplace in a purely professional one. Conversely, not all personal relationships *are* close, even if they aspire to closeness. Passionate lovers can be poles apart, however obsessive and central to their lives love is, and no one could deny that love is a personal relationship.

Two lines of reply are, I think, available to those who believe family relationships are personal but who locate personal relationships in the particularity of their participants. First, it could be suggested, that, after all, no one else but my son or my daughter could *be* my son or my daughter. The possibility of *others* having occupied these roles, which is what a merely social relationship requires, is thereby ruled out. Certainly this is true for *natural* children since they take their identity from their parentage. The possibility of adoptive children, however, makes it desirable to look to a second line of defence. This line suggests that the required particularity is provided in family relationships by the necessary place that personal history plays in it. It is just *these* people to whom I stand in a paternal relationship because, however the relationship started, it is upon these particular individuals that it is focused as it develops. The discovery that they were *not* my natural son or daughter, though no doubt horribly shocking, would not force me to rethink the relationship, as the discovery that a *soi-disant* colleague was an insane imposter would force me to rethink it.

What follows, I suggest, from this second account of personal relationships, as relationships with people as not only occupants of social roles, is a necessary condition of the personal suggested by the first account. For if I am related to a person qua particular individual and not only qua role occupant then there is no reason why my concern for them should be *restricted* to what concerns their occupancy of the role. Personal relations will not be specifically restricted in the concerns that necessarily characterize them as merely social ones are. I can be acting as a *friend* in offering financial assistance, even though it is not required of me, but I have gone beyond acting as a colleague. Herein lies, in part, the value of *personal* relationships. In them we relate to each other as persons, not merely as players of roles. This makes possible emotional *attachment* in our mutual concerns, of a sort that we contrast with the mere dutiful following out of a role's requirements. We think of concern for another as heartfelt to the extent to which it goes beyond those requirements. This is not because the 'real' person with a heart is somehow restricted by playing a role. Rather, in *personal* relations, the role *itself* is open to development in the light of the other's particularity, and not fixed independently of it. To restrict one's role to what is specifically required is to misunderstand the nature of personal relations. Indeed we might say, with only an air of paradox, that personal relationships *require* us to go beyond what they *specifically* require.

A failure to grasp this is graphically illustrated in Charles Dickens's *Dombey and Son*. Mr Dombey restricts his role as father to coldly following out its duties. Dickens displays the *impersonal* character of this relation by showing how Mr Dombey represents it as the business relationship involved in the projected firm of 'Dombey and Son'. So it is with no concern for little Paul Dombey's feelings *outside* his imagined position in the firm, that Mr Dombey accedes to Paul's request to give money to the uncle of his friend Walter Gay:

'If you had money now,' said Mr Dombey; 'as much money as young Gay talked about; what would you do?'

'Give it to his old uncle', returned Paul.

'Lend it to his old uncle, eh?' retorted Mr Dombey. 'Well! When you are old enough, you know, you will share my money, and we shall use it together.'

'Dombey and Son,' interrupted Paul, who had been tutored early in the phrase.

'Dombey and Son', repeated his father, 'Would you like to begin to be Dombey and Son now, and lend this money to young Gay's uncle?'

'Oh! if you please, Papa!' said Paul: 'and so would Florence.'

'Girls', said Mr Dombey, 'have nothing to do with Dombey and Son. Would you like it?'

'Yes, Papa, Yes!'

'Then you shall do it', returned his father. 'And you see, Paul' he added, dropping his voice, 'how powerful money is, and how anxious people are to get it. Young Gay comes all this way to beg for money, and you, who are so grand and great, having got it, are going to let him have it, as a great favour and obligation.' (Dickens, ch. 10)

As a social act, we should notice, not an act of personal friendship, of which Mr Dombey knows nothing.

Reciprocity

It is, however, to more restricted social relationships that we must turn in order to bring out some features of reciprocal relationships in general. In a wide range of social relationships we trust others to act in a certain way and, in return for their commitment to do so, commit ourselves similarly so that they can trust us. The pattern recurs among colleagues, work-mates, fellow members of associations and innumerable other partners in shared activities. There are two aspects to reciprocity which might be stressed. One is that it involves *exchange* – in the kinds of case under discussion an exchange of trust and commitment (see Becker, ch. 3). If we emphasize exchange, then we will discern reciprocity outside relationships, in, for example, the exchange of gifts or favours. We will think of reciprocity as involving a system of obligations incurred as a result of the receipt of benefits to return them in kind. And we will no doubt be reminded of the motivations for undertaking such reciprocation, suggested by equity or exchange theory (and discussed in chapter 3), namely that it provides a means whereby those involved can seek to maximize their individual benefits.

We do not need to reiterate the arguments which indicate how implausible it is to derive an account of relationships governed by norms of reciprocity from purely individualistic policies. However it is worth noting that there are relationships expressed in the reciprocal exchange of goods which cannot possibly derive from the individual's desire to maximize possession of these goods. Among the Indian peoples of British Columbia there used to be a custom of potlatch, whereby great quantities of goods, both useful and useless, were bestowed as gifts, altogether beyond what their recipients might want. And in return the recipients were expected to lavish similar extravagance upon the donors, incurring personal disadvantage thereby (cp. Lienhardt, ch. 4; Mair, (I), ch. 11). Indeed the expenditure on gifts was economically so damaging to the Indians that the colonial administration attempted to suppress the custom, which, from the standpoint of economic individualism, seemed quite irrational. Anthropologists, however, interpret potlatch and similar customs of exchange as ways of *establishing* social relationships. It seems evident that the reciprocity which characterizes these relationships does not itself, therefore, consist simply in an exchange. In so far as the parties exchange commitments to offer and return gifts this is inexplicable in terms of the value of the gifts. And yet if the point of the gift exchanges is to elicit these reciprocal commitments it is quite unclear why *this* reciprocation should constitute a relationship, if it is nothing more than a further exchange, when the original exchange of gifts did not constitute one.

The other aspect which needs stressing if we are to grasp the role of reciprocity in constituting relationships is best seen through thinking about *co-operative* activities (cp. Fried, p. 49). In a vast range of activities people work together with others to realize their individual purposes. They row in unison; they reap corn, bind sheaves and stack stooks together; they present philosophical papers, listen, criticize and respond. Unless we can rely on others to play their appointed parts in these activities we shall not be able to proceed with our own and will not attain our ends. Such activities involve reciprocity in trust and commitment – though these may be rather grandiose terms to use in this connection. But there must be a mutual recognition of individual ends, a grasp of the role each participant plays in realizing not only his own but those of others, and an attitude towards fellow participants which both relies on them to fulfil their role and justifies their reliance on others. Here we have, I suggest, a paradigm of reciprocity in co-operative activity. Stressing this aspect of reciprocity, then, would lead us to see exchange, say of gifts, as itself an activity already characterized by reciprocity: unless each could be relied upon to play their part it would not constitute exchange. So rather than exchange being the essence of reciprocity, it does itself presuppose it. Reciprocity makes possible shared activity, and it is a desire for this, not a desire for the benefits of exchange, which motivates reciprocation.

How, though, does this account explain relationships? Reciprocity, after all, exists in many contexts where relationships do not seem to be established by it: bus queues, traffic movements around roundabouts and so forth. Appearances can be deceptive, and it may be wrong to suppose that such reciprocal activity is *not* part of the network of activities that does relate us together as members of the same society: they may constitute the most general cases of social relations. But more specific relationships are formed, as I hinted earlier, by the continuing preparedness of participants to engage in reciprocal activity with more specific groups of people. Such preparedness itself involves a further layer of mutual trust and commitment, not now in relation to the *manner* of the activity but in relation to the undertaking of it. Where this mutual reliance amongst specific individuals exists over time we have relationships. We could also say that we have groups – some as small as couples – whose members are bound together by a sense of their relationship being constituted by this mutual reliance. In the next two sections I shall go on to raise some questions about the nature and value of membership of such groups.

6.2   *Collectivism and Liberal Values*

Group pressures

Social relationships of the everyday sort that I have described can seem oppressive and constricting. Why *should* I play my expected part in reciprocal activity? Why *should* I conform? Cannot relationships be spontaneous, evanescent, unsullied by troublesome expectations and embittering commitments? There are those who, by nature or from experience, are *un*clubbable, preferring to minimize their membership of groups or formal relationships because they resent being bound or beholden to others. They feel it to be an infringement of their freedom to act as they think best. Indeed the nineteenth-century sociologist Emile Durkheim argued (see Rosenberg, pp. 118–132) that such 'egoists' might even be driven to suicide by the oppression of group expectations.

Yet, in addition to 'egoist' and to 'altruist' suicide (which is undertaken precisely in order to *conform* to group expectations), Durkheim discerned a third type of suicide – 'anomic' – which arose when an individual was *too* free, *insufficiently* exposed to the pressures of group expectations. Durkheim himself thought of the influences at work here as exemplifying 'external coercion' by social facts:

a social fact is to be recognised by the power of external coercion which it exercises or is capable of exercising over individuals, and the presence of the power may be recognised in its turn either by the existence of some specific sanction or by resistance offered against every individual effort that tends to violate it. (Durkheim, p. 10)

He thought that this sort of 'coercion' was opaque to individuals. They simply felt the pressure without having any grasp of what *reasons* there might be for them to succumb to it. They might have an affectual attachment to the social group which coerces them, but this affection is blind to what is good about the group. And analogously, that such pressures were, as he thought, necessary to a satisfactory life, and the lack of them a cause of anomie, was a sociologically observed fact without a rational justification. According to this approach to social explanation there just are certain norms of behaviour adherence to which is required by one's social group. In the case of many groups, especially in primitive societies, these will be norms of reciprocal behaviour. But once we have identified these 'social facts' there is no more to be said to explain action in conformity with them. Evidently this Durkheimian kind of account will not appeal to those who seek an *understanding* of social relationships from a participant's standpoint. In particular we seek this because as participants we may wish to criticize and revise these relationships, and to do so, not just because they conduce to social integration or disintegration (in the ways that Durkheim notices), but because they seem unreasonable or repugnant (see ch. 8.3).

Groups constituted by reciprocal activity have, in particular, attracted criticism as tending to hamper individual liberty. That I am bound to act in certain ways which are expected of me by others, who bind themselves to act similarly to me, seems to restrict both my freedom to do as I wish and theirs. In these circumstances the individual seems to be dominated by the group, as much as if he were dominated by another individual who put him under oppressive obligations as a condition of satisfying some of his interests within a relationship. If then, as I have hinted, reciprocity between individuals is an alternative to power struggles, it may not be a preferable alternative, since a struggle for power has re-emerged between the individual and the group.

To this it may be countered that in many and arguably all groups constituted by reciprocal activity there is an element of collective decision-making in which the individual group member has a role. In some it will be direct, so that each member has a say in the organization of activity; in others indirect, so that he only chooses those who do the organizing. In still others, collective decisions may be so ossified that little decision-*making* goes on in any explicit way; though even here the willingness or unwillingness of members to participate will enable them

to influence group activity. In all, it would appear, there is scope for
some individual freedom to decide how the group should act. And this
will distinguish such groups from those constituted simply out of power
relations.

Yet the critic of reciprocal groups will find scant consolation here.
Collective decisions themselves, it will be said, bind members of the
group to courses of action they might not have chosen otherwise, and
this impairs their freedom to do what they want. 'Such control', it is
suggested

> is voluntarily accepted in some religious orders, but it conspicuously
> involves the surrender of personal autonomy and the renunciation of the
> will.... Whether consciously or not, it is such ideals that influence
> present day secular and sectarian groups whose desire to eliminate the
> individual is based on some much more tenuous theoretical background
> .... The burden of individual choice is submerged in the collective will.
> (Cohen, pp. 23–4)

This kind of complaint throws up a conflict between, on the one hand,
liberalism, which emphasizes the value of individual freedom, and, on
the other, collectivism, which emphasizes that of commitment to, and
integration in, the group. While collectivism can take a conservative
form which turns for exemplars of reciprocity to traditional societies, it
is its socialist form that tends to arouse controversy. For here we seem
to have a contemporary clash between liberal and socialist values.

Liberal social and political thought attaches overriding importance to
the freedom of the individual to act only from considerations that relate
to the advancing of individual – but not necessarily his own – interests.
The nineteenth-century liberal theorist Jeremy Bentham believed that
'individual interests are the only real interests', implying that 'if anything has value at all, the value must accrue to someone, somewhere in
the form of an actual human experience' (Sabine, pp. 745–6). It is by
reference to one's own sense of which experiences one likes and which
one does not that one judges the benefits of a practice or policy. Thus
liberals emphasize, in particular, the value of autonomy – the individual's ability to live in such a way that one's actions are those that one
thinks best according to one's own lights. For without autonomy one
will not be free to act only from consideration of individual interests as
one judges them. The kind of individualism involved here is not necessarily the psychological individualism of Hobbes, which holds that only
individual interests *are* motivating. Instead it is a *moral* individualism

(cp. Graham, (BD), pp. 98–9) which holds that only individual interests *should* motivate, and that therefore people should be free from pressures to act otherwise than from consideration of them.

Liberal thought, accordingly, finds collective activity unjustifiable. And this is the charge levelled in particular against collective enterprises like trade unionism. In a trade union people often seem to act blindly, carried along on the emotions of a mass meeting. They do things against their own interests and apparently against the interests of others. Individuals are submerged in the mass so that they seem to consult neither conscience nor prudence. Such behaviour seems to the liberal to epitomize collective action and to be a denial of autonomy.

How can collectivists reply to this criticism? One kind of reply draws attention to cases of collective action which seem incontestably rational. Those bands of reapers, binders and stackers of corn working together provided an efficient way of getting the harvest in before mechanization. Individuals working alone ran the risk of the cut corn being soaked on the ground by a summer shower. More generally, activities performed by a group, in which each member plays his or her allotted role, may be more efficient in realizing individual ends than those in which individuals set to work by themselves. The essence of reciprocal activity is not that it involves actions performed *with* other people, but actions co-ordinated with theirs through reciprocated trust and commitment. Now, the collectivist may say, the liberal can have no objection to this kind of *instrumental* reciprocity (cp. Gould, pp. 72–4), since it is entered into precisely to satisfy individual interests and involves no limitations on individual freedom beyond what is required for this goal.

If the liberal replies that not all reciprocal activity is of this type, but that some is entered into for ends other than the advancement of individual interests, some proponents of collective action may simply claim that the liberal is mistaken. Such a collectivist will deny that there is a clash of *values* between liberals, and, say, socialists. He will deny then that there are distinctively *socialist* values (cp. Collier, (S)). Socialists, he will say, differ from liberals, not in holding that there are reasons for collective action over and above the satisfaction of individual interests and the preservation of individual freedom, but in holding that collective action is required to accomplish this in far more cases than the liberal recognizes: 'for this argument about liberty and collectivism is a case of practical reasoning in which one position with definite practical consequences – liberalism – is criticised, not in the name of different values, but of an explanatory theory about human life and society' (Collier, (P), p. 43).

The force of this response on behalf of collectivism is to defuse the liberal charge that individual interests and freedoms become submerged in the interests and aims of the group in collective action. In doing so it denies that there is an *distinctive* value in actions where individual concerns are, to some extent, subordinated to the concerns of the group. Yet it is far from clear that those who engage in collective action do not, at least sometimes, act out of a conviction that there *is* such a value. The combine harvester has taken over the work of the reapers, binders and stackers of stooks, but there are those who regret these changes, while conceding the combine's greater efficiency in serving individual interests. Nor is it just that elusive benefit to the individual – company – which is thought to have been lost, for that can be had during increased leisure hours; rather it is a feature of the relationships with others involved in reciprocal activity. Thus when people prefer to discuss philosophy together it is not that they prefer to do in company what they could do on their own. Nor yet that they necessarily think they will get on better with others than on their own; indeed they may accept that their own researches may not be advanced, or may even be impeded by it. Rather it is because they value the way in which they can achieve a common purpose – which may not have been the original purpose of any of them – through the give and take of group discussion. To remind us of the role of the common purpose we may call this kind of reciprocity *communal* reciprocity (cp. Gould, pp. 76–7).

What have been termed socialist – or more generally collectivist – values are held to reside in relationships characterized by communal reciprocity. These are relationships participated in freely by members who have a sufficient regard for the group's interest in pursuing a purpose common to all that they are prepared, on occasion, to subordinate their individual interests to it. It is in principle possible, therefore, that the interests of the group will be preferred even to the interests of a majority of members. Evidently a group characterized by relations of reciprocity, such as a trade union, will flourish in the long term only if its members' interests are served. But a particular section or even a whole cohort of members may suffer in respect of their individual interests in order to further that of the group, as when, for example, a trade union would be permanently damaged by a climbdown over a pay claim. And in all cases we can draw a distinction between members' interests as individuals and their interests as a group. It is the latter that members are concerned with. So, though they have faith that group membership is good for the totality of members, it is not the totality of members' interests which are the object of their regard, but the interests of the group. The group is what they value, not for the further good it brings its members, but for the good that membership is viewed as being in itself. In 6.3 I shall look more closely at the nature of collective decision-making in such a group, and at the kind of value that participation might have. But first I want to return to the liberal criticism of communal reciprocity.

Individual autonomy

Where reciprocal relationships cannot be justified solely as instrumental in satisfying individual interests the liberal will regard them as irrational. But this objection need cut no ice with the collectivist, who believes that the furtherance of group interests is also a worthwhile aim. What the liberal must do, then, is to attack communal reciprocity as destructive of values the collectivist does cherish. He does so, as we have seen, by alleging that communal reciprocity involves an unnecessary restriction on individual autonomy. Now this charge has several strands which need to be disentangled. The first consists in the objection that collective action commonly involves individuals doing what they do not want to do and cannot justify, but which they do do for fear of expulsion from the group or other sanctions. Non-collective action by contrast need put no one in this position. Yet, conversely, non-collective action may analogously involve people not doing what they *do* want to do, namely participate in reciprocal relations with others, like the reapers overtaken by farm machinery, and this may outweigh the disbenefits. Only an argument to the effect that wanting this cannot be justified will serve the liberal here.

Liberals argue, however, in a second and related objection, that collective action should generally be avoided since it saddles individuals with *responsibility* for acts they might individually think unjustified. While it is admitted that I might sometimes have an interest in participating in collective decisions, where I do not it is unreasonable to put myself into a position of assuming responsibility. The objection is, then, to long-term relationships characterized by collective reciprocity. Yet surely the objection proves too much. For membership of *any* group, however constituted, would be objectionable on these principles, assuming that the group was one that I was free to leave at will. On this condition I would bear *some* responsibility for the actions of the group if I chose to remain a member. I might minimize the risk of being held personally responsible for its actions, but that looks like *evading* one's responsibility rather than remaining morally in the clear.

However, in a third, and seemingly inconsistent, line of attack, liberals object to participation in collective action as a device whereby individuals actually *escape* personal responsibility. Collective action, they claim, does not allow the clear ascription of responsibility to individuals, to whom alone it could properly belong and without which they will not be properly autonomous. Yet this objection ignores the fact that in *making* collective decisions individuals do *do* something. It is from their participation in this process that an individual's responsibility for collective acts derives.

This leads, though, to a fourth and more subtle liberal objection to collective action. It is that, rather than infringing the individual's freedom to do what they do want, it undermines the very *formation* of individual desires, and hence the *acceptance* of individual responsibility for participation in collective actions. In a word, it undermines autonomy, through weakening the disposition to act by one's own lights. Now this criticism is sometimes expressed as if it were founded on empirical observation of the baneful psychological effects of membership of reciprocal groups. This is not to be taken too seriously. Second-hand dreams and their concomitant flights from *serious* decision-taking are so common that it would be propagandist to attribute more of them to the traditional trade unionist than to the competitive entrepreneur, even though the former takes many work-place decisions collectively and the latter does not. Both may, for example, plead the inevitability of circumstances or the expectations of others as excuses for their acts.

The liberal objection is more properly a philosophical one and needs to be assessed as such. It depends upon the claim that to act on a collective decision is not to act from a desire springing from one's own standards of desirability. What one gives as a reason for one's act need not be a reason from which one would act *outside* the arena of collective decision, *outside* of action in the relationship characterized by communal reciprocity. In that case, says the liberal, one's action must be explained by capitulation to pressures to conform. To act thus is to act as if one were not free to do otherwise, since one's own individual desires are irrelevant to how one acts. In these circumstances one need form no individual desires, and consequently feel no individual responsibility for one's act, which is the very antithesis of being autonomous, namely *heteronomous* – acting in accordance with principles other than one's own (cp. Benn, p. 176).

The criticism is a powerful one, since it rests on the perception that in acting collectively I am doing *more* than adhering to the principle that I shall normally act on collective decisions even when I disagree with them. For I might adopt that principle simply by weighing my desire for continued membership of the group against the unfavourable features of the act and I would not need to adopt it if expulsion was unlikely. The criticism notices, as is surely sometimes true, that I *subordinate* my own judgement itself to the collective decision. I accept the decision as the *right* one to act upon, rather than simply putting up with it as the one I must act on to satisfy my other desires (e.g. for 'company').

It would be foolish to deny that there are cases in which those taking collective action do so through fear of reprisals or docile habits of conformity. But equally there are those who do so in the belief that they are doing right. They act from loyalty, from a sense of commitment. Is acting from such a motive heteronomous? I do not see that it is. For although the participant in collective action does not need to decide that his action is right because it serves individual interests, he decides that it is right because it is of a kind that he does value, namely participation in collective action that furthers the interests of the group. Now valuing *that* is not making a judgement borrowed from the group; the judgement is the individual's own. The collectivist is acting according to his own lights in accepting the decision of the group as the right one to act upon. Although under the description 'stopping work' he may not think some action is desirable, under the description 'showing solidarity with fellow workers' he may think that it is. And upon consideration of the pros and cons he opts for following the collective decision. Accordingly, the collectivist can be as autonomous as the liberal.

6.3 *Fraternity*

Rousseau and the general will

Yet, even if it is accepted that the collectivist can be acting by his own lights in going along with group decisions, the liberal will still be uneasy. For has it not been conceded that the collectivist none the less *subordinates* his own personal view of what should be done to the decision of the group? Indeed that he does this is the price to be paid for group membership. But is it not too high a price to pay, unless it serves to maximize the number of group members who *do* find that the decision of the group is in accordance with their views, as, for example, should happen in *democratic* groups?

Such a conclusion mistakes the collectivist's account of what involvement in collective decision-making involves. In this process, claims the collectivist, we participate not by offering our *personal* views on what should be done, but rather our views *as members* of the group.

The distinction between my personal view and my view as a member of a group was given its classic exposition by the eighteenth-century

French thinker Jean-Jacques Rousseau. In considering the community as a whole as a social group he wrote:

> There is often a considerable difference between the will of all and the general will. The latter is concerned only with the common interest, the former with interests that are partial, being itself but the sum of individual wills. (Rousseau, p. 274)

What he means is that a body of people considering only their own individual interests may arrive at a judgement of what to do – the will of all – which may not in fact be in the common interest (choosing more private cars, perhaps, rather than better public transport). If, on the other hand, each thinks of himself only as a representative member of the group, forgetting his particular and private interests, then a decision made on this basis – the general will – should serve the common interest (assuming it is technically sound as to the means to be employed). In general, Rousseau believes that this will turn out to be the case anyway, because particular private interests cancel each other out. But this should not obscure the fact that members who approach collective decision-making with private interests in mind adopt the wrong attitude. Then as he says:

> Each, separating his interests and the interests of all, sees that such separation cannot be complete, yet the part he plays in the general damage seems to him as nothing compared with the exclusive good which he seeks to appropriate. With the single exception of the particular private benefit at which he aims, he still desires the public good, realising that it is likely to benefit him every whit as much as his neighbours.... The fault that he commits is to change the form of the question, and to answer something he was not asked. Thus, instead of saying, through the medium of his vote, 'this is of advantage to the State,' he says, 'it is to the advantage of this or that individual that such and such a proposition become law.' (Rousseau, p. 386)

Individuals ought to participate, then, in a way that considers, not their own individual interests, but that of the group, and on the assumption that others will do the same. It would be irrational to participate otherwise (cp. Barnard, pp. 141–2).

This is a point that liberal theorists persistently fail to acknowledge. They interpret participation in deliberating upon collective decisions as if it were a matter of exchanging *personal* opinions on what should be done and reaching a decision on the basis of what the majority would prefer to happen. They assume, of course, that I could always coherently form a view about this outside of membership of a group, and that group organization simply collects and mediates between these different opinions. Forms of decision-making best suited to the democratic processing of personal opinions, such as postal ballots for trade unionists, are advocated by liberals, in preference, say, to mass meetings where, it is feared, participants will not express their 'true opinions'. The liberal theorist assumes that this must happen as a result of intimidation or other pressures to conform, because he sees that the views aired at such meetings are often not those expressed outside the collective situation. It is a commonplace that workers often condemn other workers for striking while voicing enthusiasm for striking themselves in an analogous situation. Yet this is because the participant in a collective decision rightly regards it as *irrelevant* to form a personal opinion on what should be done. The participant speaks only as a group member bearing in mind only what will advance the interests of the group. So the fact that the views aired at mass meetings may differ from those expressed elsewhere need not be due to illegitimate pressures.

Collective decision-making determines certain criteria as to what will be relevant contributions to discussion, contributions that flow from concern for the interests of the group, which depend upon its more or less explicit objectives. In the case of a trade union these are the protection and improvement of members' terms and conditions of employment. These rule out some matters as even topics for discussion. For instance a trade union, unlike the army, forms no view on the private sexual behaviour of members. Thus some considerations are irrelevant to discussion as not bearing on the union's objectives, for example the chances of members being thrown together as sexual partners. Although we are told that the objects of early trade clubs were 'firstly – and most importantly – to buy beer and have cheerful evenings (Cole and Postgate, p. 166), this may not be as irrelevant to fostering collective action as may appear.

Immediately it can be seen, however, that *irrelevant* considerations may weigh with some members in forming a *personal* opinion of the best outcome. For such an opinion would have to take account of *all* the interests of the individual and of others for whom he has some concern. If his concerns are altruistic he will take account of all the interests of other members, and this is how participation in collective action contrary to one's individual interests is sometimes presented. But this is quite misconceived. It is no more my business to take account of others' interests where these do not bear on the objectives of the group than to take account of my own. I am concerned with their interests only *as* fellow members, not as people whose lives I happen to be able to affect through membership of the same group.

The picture I am presenting is of a *discipline* of thought and action imposed by mutual adherence to the group's objectives and common commitment to the group's way of attaining them. If each person simply formed a personal opinion on what should be done, then all that would bind him to the collective view would be fear of sanctions or emotional attachment to the group. But this is not to undertake the kind of discipline that characterizes a relationship in which trust and commitment are reciprocated. For this, the participant must ally himself with the judgements of what is desirable that are determined by the group, rather than acting on those he would have followed had he not been a member of the group. And he must be able to trust others to do likewise; or else he can have no confidence that his own interests as a group member will be duly considered.

We can now say something more positive about the value of this discipline in the life of the individual by way of an antidote to the liberal charge that collective action undermines individual autonomy. What group membership forces us to do is to justify our assessment of something's value in contributing to collective decisions. Now acceptance of the need to do this is, I suggest, necessary for me to claim any authority for my own judgements of value. Without it my desires would simply be facts about me, which neither I nor others could view as the apprehension of what is really desirable (cp. 2.5). For the desirability of a thing is a reason not just for me but for others to have it, so that to justify my desire is to get another to recognize that desirability and hence have a goal in common with me. There is no reason to think that such agreement would be possible outside of all social relationships in which our concerns were comparable. Indeed the justification of our evaluative judgements typically takes place within such relationships. In them I am held responsible for what I do and have to justify to others the judgements that my actions rest upon. The *abstract* notion of responsibility used in liberal theory neglects these concrete surroundings, in which we are answerable for our acts.

The value of relationships for the individual is, in part, that they permit the validation of his individual judgements. To *reject* their discipline is not to resist the disintegration of individual desire, which the liberal fears, but its rational integration into social life. On the collectivist view 'morality begins', as Durkheim suggested, 'with life in the group, since it is only there that disinterestedness and devotion become meaningful' (quoted Munch, p. 127).

Fraternal feelings

Social relations of the sort that regulate the actions of the participants independently of their individual interests, but in virtue of the collective pursuit of a common interest, may, when they are not personal relations, be thought of as *fraternal* ones. Fraternity (the word is intended without any implications as to the gender of those to whom it relates, is a relation existing between those engaged collectively in achieving a common purpose. This common purpose is essential to the relation of fraternity, for without it there is nothing to delimit the expectations and commitments which define the relation.

To suppose there could be fraternity without a common purpose and a collective pursuit of it is once more to mistake a generalized altruism for attachment to the common interest. So it is wrong to suggest that 'the subjective feeling of fraternity is that of brotherhood: the objective behaviour is that of altruism', (Halsey, p. 11) and to go on to suspect (ibid., p. 161) that class divisions undermine fraternity as a national bond because they limit the scope of altruism. Certainly class divisions would undermine fraternity, but that is because they produce conflicts between the common interests of different groups. The point was appreciated not only by Marx (quoted Peters, (E), p. 219), who said that only in the working class was 'the true brotherhood of man' to be found, but also by conservative thinkers (e.g. Sir James Fitzjames Stephen, p. 287). It might not be unfair to suggest that liberals are attracted to the idea of brotherhood to the degree to which common interests, and hence effective organization in pursuit of them, are *not* demonstrable; as when it is said, 'the feeling of fraternity must at least be attached to the kinship of being a person (Peters, (E), p. 225). In my view it can be *least* attached to that.

Hazy ideas about the brotherhood of man are perhaps encouraged by the fact that fraternity is a relationship characterized by *feelings*. But only a false conception of feelings as experiences we could in principle share, whatever our actual relationship, would lead to the view that we could extend out fraternal relationships indefinitely. In fact the feelings involved in fraternal relations only count as fraternal if those I have them towards are, or are imagined to be, related by common interest. The feelings of fraternity are the feelings of trust and commitment towards those engaged in the collective pursuit of this interest.

We value fraternity, as we do friendship and love. The fact that we do indicates the value that we attach to reciprocal relationships, which is, I have suggested, the value of pursuing common goals. Without them we must be in doubt of the value of pursuing our own. I want to re-emphasize that this is not just a matter of fellow feeling, of the comfort of kinship with others. It is good to have the sympathy and support of others in a similar situation to oneself. But this is not yet to recognize a *common* interest. That comes only with the possibility of collective action, when those involved acquire a different structure, the structure of a group.

Sartre, in his later work, *Critique of Dialectical Reason*, tells a similar story (book II, chs 1 and 2) of how those with the same individual interests (e.g. people standing at a bus queue) can become 'fused' into a group with a common interest. They become a group because they recognize that each has an interest in promoting the others' interests as well as their own, since in getting what serves their interests they stand together. The distinction between individual interest and common interest becomes blurred. Outside of the immediate situation in which this fusion occurs, however, the group may well dissolve. The group survives its original creation only through the exchange of 'pledges' of collective action. But Sartre thinks that what then links the members is a 'fraternity of fear'. Where my account differs from Sartre's is in trying to find *value* in membership. Without it our feeling of fraternity would be unintelligible to us. With it we do not need to look to fear as a motive (though we shall return to fear as social cement in the next chapter).

6.4   *Love as a Social Relation*

I started this chapter by contrasting personal and merely social relations. I now want to suggest that *personal* relations can have the same structure of reciprocity as the merely social ones typified by trade union membership and the like. Surprisingly enough, this seems most evidently the case with sexual love.

Love should be thought of as principally a certain reciprocal relation, although of course it is not always reciprocated. But the lover is one who seeks to initiate or sustain this relation. Only through an understanding of what the relationship requires can they do so. I have argued that the demands of sexual desire cannot reveal these requirements: it generates no pattern of mutual expectations and commitments. Nor does the desire for power.

It may seem that love is a form of friendship. But though love is often *accompanied* by friendship, it is hard to see how love as such could be a form of it; for sexual desire can play nothing but an accidental role in friendship. Sexual relations are, at most, a means whereby the mutual companionship and support of friendship may be furthered: they do not exemplify such companionship and support, as they exemplify the bonds of love. Similarly the fraternity of trade unionists is not a form of friendship, since their specific objective – the improvement of their working lives – is not an example of any benefit whose pursuit is essential to friendship. Friends could be uninterested in this aspect of each others' lives, and those who were interested *only* in this aspect would not, so far, be friends,

Yet in a relationship of sexual love there is a specific objective analogous to that of trade unionists: it is the mutual satisfaction of sexual desire. That this is given as a common purpose is what makes the relationship sexual love. It is right to give it priority, but wrong to think that love thereby becomes a *form* of sexual desire, any more than trade unionism is a form of discontent with one's work, just because it aims to mitigate it. In each case the relationship may be motivated by these individual feelings. But, in both, individual interests are subordinated to a *common* goal. In this respect love differs from the project of desire in which each participant is overridingly concerned to satisfy their own sexual urges, if necessary by the manipulation of the other's desire whether they wish it or not. In love the carrying out of the project is to be by means of a commitment to the principle that what is done should result from shared desire. The value that is set on this overrides the value set on satisfying individual desire. If this were not so then whenever prudential considerations indicated that the relationship was not maximally conducive to individual satisfaction it would be rational to terminate it. Yet it is evident that lovers take no such view of the value of their love and (if my arguments in 6.3 have force) it is not clear that they are wrong.

Again I want to say that the value attached to fulfilling a common purpose does not derive from altruism towards one's partner. Lovers are not concerned with what is best for each other – which may well be some *other* relationship! – but what is best for them *as a couple*. This conception cannot be derived from somehow adding concern for another to concern for oneself. It arises only if one can conceive of the common purpose to which each party subordinates their individual interests. The reciprocity which the later Sartre looked for to resolve the power struggle of love (see 5.4) is, I suggest, to be found in the way in which this common purpose is pursued collectively. The lovers set out to achieve this goal which, though it serves the interest they share as a couple, is pursued disinterestedly, with a view only to mutual satisfaction. Love, surprisingly, is in this way *impersonal*, realized through the performance of roles, rather than the unconstrained expression of personality. But then all reciprocal relations, personal or not, must share this character.

If this sounds as if it excludes the centrality of *feeling* in love it should be recalled that what counts as a certain kind of feeling can depend upon the sort of social relation in which it figures. The phenomenology of the feelings of love do, I believe, reflect the sort of relation I have claimed love is. The feelings of love depend on valuing the reciprocal achievement of a common purpose. They are sexual feelings, but (as Freud noted; see 2.3) not uninhibitedly so. The lover cannot press on unrestrainedly to that goal: the response of the beloved is sought. So, in the longings of love, the lover's anxiety is at the failure or loss of such mutuality. These emotions do not move one to bring about a definite outcome, to make things happen which might force the pace in a way unresponsive to the beloved. Yet nor are the longings of love feelings of dissatisfaction that what one wants has not transpired. Feelings of fulfilment in love are, correspondingly, not feelings of satisfaction, but rather of shared desire and activity. Yet pre-eminently feelings of love are feelings of trust and commitment; for the sharing of desire and activity is an achievement, not an accident. It is something accomplished through the lovers setting a value on it and resolving to pursue it reciprocally. The feelings that are antithetical to love, feelings of power, of dependence, of disloyalty or of jealousy, spring from breakdowns in the reciprocity which constitutes love.

Even if this account allows for emotion, however, can it take care of the *personal* nature of love? Three points of objection might be made to the account. First, surely I do not value love because it makes possible the joint pursuit of a worthwhile common purpose. I value not love in *general* but love of a *particular* person, and I value it *on his account*. Second and connectedly, I love my lover for *himself*, not because he happens to be my lover. Third, I am concerned for my lover's interests *as a person*, not just those he has in virtue of being my lover and thus sharing a common purpose; and I expect an analogous attitude from him.

All these points may, I think, be granted without conceding that the account of love as a social relation is mistaken. They bring out, rather, that it is a social relation of an essentially personal character. To take the first point. Of course I do not look for just *anyone* who will embark with me on a shared project of mutual satisfaction, or, if I did, it would not be from love that I did so. What I value is loving *him*, not just anyone or anyone of a specific sort. And this is because in love the beloved's lovable features are appreciated as those of a particular person who matters to me independently of my antecedent interests or valuations. It follows, to take the second point, that I love him for himself, not just in virtue of a role he fills. The latter would be possible only if the value of love did lie in sustaining this kind of relationship with someone or other, rather than with a particular person. The third point which draws attention to the *generalized* well-being that is sought in love recalls the necessary condition for *personal* relationships discussed in 6.1. Because I love a particular person whose individual interests and valuations concern me, not just the holder of a role whose do not, my relations with him are not confined to the sexual project. For though, I claim, a focus on sex is what constitutes the relation as sexual love, how the project expands will be a matter for the lovers to determine, in their role as lovers. In love it is not enough that a *modus vivendi* be agreed between partners in which some individual desires get satisfied and others do not. While in fraternal relationships generally individual desires do, I have argued, get modified as members ally themselves to the purposes of the group, in love the modification of individual desires themselves is positively required (though it does not happen without a struggle).

What seems distinctive of love is the way this comes about through the shaping of desires initially indeterminate into a distinctive project suffused with sexuality but variously focused on specific sexual goals. This indeterminacy is readily intelligible in the light of the lovers' relationship, for determinacy would impede the openness to the other's contribution to the project which is required. We have, then, in love a common purpose consisting, not of miraculously compatible desires and interests pre-formed, but of aims determined through the course of the social relation. So in love we do not have a sense of determinate goals to be achieved, but of possibilities that are both exciting and frightening, whereby our desires become determinate.

This helps to explain, I suggest, why love does not present itself to lovers with the perspicuous structure that fraternity presents to trade unionists, for example. Its common purpose is plastic and consequentially inexplicit. Nor therefore can there be formal processes of collective decision-making for bringing it about. What lovers look for is rather an area of shared feeling through which a common purpose can be determined and pursued without apparent regulation. These features of the relationship disguise its abstract similarity to more formal and more explicit examples of communal reciprocity.

In the next chapter we shall compare and contrast the claims of power relations and of reciprocal relations to be what constitute society.

Anyway, whatever else is the case, Freud was surely wrong in thinking that what binds us to other members of our society is that we share a kind of *love* for those who lead us!

Further reading

The distinction between the public and the private is explored in S. I. Benn and G. F. Gauss (eds) *Public and Private in Social Life* (especially chapters 1–7 and 12). The distinction has many applications to the way we live our lives. But do we need it and if so why?

The threat to autonomy from collective action is discussed in S. I. Benn *A Theory of Freedom* (chapter 12) and debated between Cohen and Collier in 'Positive Values'. Evidently there must be limits beyond which collective organization is undoubtedly oppressive. What are they and how are they determined? A good general treatment of the individualism versus collectivism controversy is Gordon Graham's *Contemporary Social Philosophy* (especially chapters 1 and 2).

Rousseau's *The Social Contract* is required reading. To what extent can the common interest and the interest of all in a group part company? Keith Graham's *The Battle of Democracy* (chapter 6) is a useful discussion of collective action. The claims of larger groups (e.g. the community as a whole) to regulate collective action by smaller groups (e.g. trade unions) are, of course, a major source of political controversy. How *should* we integrate our different roles?

It is worth wondering how many kinds of personal relation have a common purpose and reciprocal methods for achieving it. What might the common purpose of *friendship* be? Or how might reciprocity be involved in love between parents and the children they bring up?

7

Society and the State

7.1 *Terror and Government*

A brutish state of nature?

What *kind* of relationship, we can now ask, binds men and women together into societies, that is to say, into the sorts of comprehensive social groups in which people live together everywhere? Three candidates present themselves. There are those relationships, if any, which spring directly from our biological nature. There are those that, unquestionably, result from the exercise of power by some at the expense of others. And finally there are those which, I argued in the last chapter, stem from the co-operative pursuit of common purposes.

An obvious answer might seem to be that each kind of relationship makes a contribution to the web of social connections that constitutes society. We have (in chapter 2), however, had reason to doubt the general efficacy of sociobiology in explaining our social relationships as we ordinarily conceive of them. No doubt there are facts about human natural history which enable us to live together as we do: *certain* tendencies to intra-species aggression are lacking, for example. But these facts do not appear to produce the highly specific forms of social organization that are found among some other animals. Thomas Hobbes, in appreciating how different we are from ants and bees in this regard, denies man's *natural* sociality, in the biological sense. But this leads him on also to deny that human relationships can be conceived in terms of the advancement of irreducibly social goods, such as co-operation and harmony seem to be. This is because he cannot see how these goods could motivate people, unless our propensity to pursue them over individual interests was overridden by biological drives to sociability.

Thomas Hobbes, whose individualist theory we have looked at earlier
(3.1), was in no doubt that an account of society needed to be provided
which showed how social relationships and institutions served the purposes of individuals, and remained in place precisely because they served
them well. Socialization involved the application of mechanisms whereby it was in the interests of individuals to live together in society.
Without such mechanisms they would have no motive for doing so.

Hobbes argued that in a state of nature there is a 'warre of every man
against every man' in which individuals are literally fighting for survival,
for safety and for superiority. Hobbes thought that the only escape
from this situation was for people to agree to place themselves under
'such a Common Power, as may be able to defend themselves from the
invasion of Forraigners, and the injuries of one another, and thereby to
secure them in such sort, as that by their owne industrie, and by the
fruites of the Earth, they may nourish themselves and live contentedly'
(Hobbes, ch. 17). It is fear of this power that binds people together as
fellow members of society, each having the same interest in ensuring
that the laws of government are obeyed, so that other members cannot
threaten them. The relationships constitutive of society, then, are for
Hobbes essentially *political* ones, ones that reflect shared subordination
to the power of government. The idea that conflict is *natural* to human
beings can derive from two sources. Irrespective of the source it will
seem, as for Hobbes, that government is necessary for society as what
restrains conflict. The first possible source is aggressive instincts and the
like. On this view, conflict inevitably arises from man's biological make-
up, because facts about human nature alone determine that human
beings will fight each other. Sometimes this view is argued for on the
grounds that aggression is evolutionarily adaptive. This has all the weaknesses of sociobiological explanations noted in chapter 2. There is no
way of showing *what* features have enabled us to survive evolutionarily:
so evolutionary theory gives no grounds for thinking that aggression is
biologically necessary to us, and hence none for thinking that it is
indeed a feature of our *biological* make-up. Furthermore, what can be
shown to be genetically determined are specific patterns of behaviour.
What counts as 'conflict' or 'violence', however, is very various in its
causes, forms and consequences. A world war is a very different thing
from a bar-room brawl. There is therefore no reason for regarding
conflict as a biological feature of human life which must be given a
genetic explanation.

Hobbes himself is not arguing that conflict is natural in this first
sense. Rather, he thinks that it is natural in the sense that it is the *normal*
state of things unless prevented. And this is not because we are speci-

fically motivated towards conflict by aggressive instincts. Instead it is because the *conditions* for conflict normally exist, namely lack of adequate resources to satisfy our ordinary drives permanently. Hobbes thinks, then, that in the absence of restraints we have good reason to engage in conflict to serve our individual interests. What would need a special explanation in terms of our nature would be the *absence* of conflict. It is this which he notices among ants and bees by contrast with human beings and for which he thinks a biological explanation must be forthcoming.

Yet what kind of empirical evidence is there for agreeing with Hobbes that without political organization 'warre' would result? Hobbes notes that:

> It may peradventure be thought, there was never such a time, nor condition of warre as this: and I believe it was never generally so, over all the world: but there are many places, where they live so now. For the savage people in many places of *America*, except the government of small Families, the concord whereof dependeth on naturall lust, have no government at all; and live at this day in that brutish manner, as I said before. Howsoever, it may be perceived what manner of life there would be, where there were no common Power to feare: by the manner of life, which men that have formerly lived under a peacefull government, use to degenerate into, in a civill Warre. (Hobbes, ch. 13)

We shall return (in 7.3) to Hobbes's account of Red Indians. But first let us look at his paradigm of the state of nature – civil war. Many philosophers think of the outbreak of civil war or of terrorism as somehow evidence for Hobbes's account of why government is necessary to society. One suggests that the only way to convince Hobbes's opponent is to invite him to 'live in a country where authority has disappeared ... he will soon discover the meaning and prescience of Hobbes's gloomy imaginings. I lived', he reports, 'for a month in Ireland in 1922. There was no actual loss of life near us during that time, only a few shots audible in the night. Yet there was fear and suspicion everywhere and all peaceful avocations had come to an end. Fear and veiled hostility had destroyed the whole structure of social life' (Mabbott, pp. 21–2). Or similarly another:

> every political community has understood that random and indiscriminate violence is the ultimate threat to social cohesion, and thus every political community has some form of prohibition against it. Terrorism allowed full sway would reduce civil society to the state of nature where there is in Hobbes' fine description, 'continual fear of violent death, and the life of

man, poor, nasty, brutish, and short.' No political society can sanction
terrorism, for that would be a self-contradiction, as the very reasons for
entering civil society were to escape precisely those conditions imposed by
the terrorist. (Phillips, p. 89)

It is anxieties of this sort that lead politicians to talk of waging 'a war
against terrorism', in order to defend society itself. But it is important to
notice that on this account it must not really be a *war* that the government wages against its internal adversaries, since this would plunge the
community into precisely that 'warre of every man against every man'
that terrifies Hobbesians and from which it is the role of government to
save us. Rather, terrorist activity must be suppressed, in just the way
that other *criminal* activity must be, through the application of the law.
Rebellion against the government is just an extreme case of any breaches
of the law, all of which threaten internal order by manifesting disobedience and unrestrained individual interest.

We should note, however, that civil war provides evidence of social
breakdown only if it is *assumed* that a society is co-terminous with the
state in conflict. Yet in actual civil wars there is, after all, much social
organization remaining rather than only warring individuals: in particular that which licenses us to speak of different 'sides' in the conflict, as
well as the relations which continue to unite civilians on both sides.
Clear-sighted empirical observation of civil war or terrorism really does
not establish that all social organization depends upon subordination to
the government of a state.

It simply is not true that insurrection or terrorism lead remorselessly
to the breakdown of social life. Terrorism is a threat, not to society
itself, but to particular social organizations. Hobbes's empirical grounds
for his theory of the inevitability of conflict in the absence of governmental restraints are, then, unconvincing. As a result his view of social
relations as utterly dependent upon government is not persuasive.

The brutish nature of the state?

But could Hobbes's be right? Could society really be thought of as
constituted by subordination to the power of government? Hobbes
presents the exercise of government power against insurrectionaries as
somehow *justified* by its defence of society. Yet if society were *simply* a
state of subjection to superior force, it seems hard to see why it should
not eventually arise quite naturally from the triumph of one power over
others. And this would do nothing to justify the triumphant power in
its continued exercise of force.

The charge is in effect that the government acts no differently from its violent opponents: it aims to impose its will on others by waging, or threatening to wage, a kind of war against them; this is not peace and harmony, but terror and oppression. This view has had supporters from both right and left. The nineteenth-century conservative thinker Herbert Spencer held that 'government is begotten of aggression and by aggression,' so that 'the ethics of Government, originally identical with the ethics of war, must long remain akin to them' (Spencer, pp. 54–5). Spencer's point is that government arises 'where successful aggression ends in subjection of neighbouring tribes'. But the aggressive character of government is in no way confined to the 'internal inequities' of conquerors, or those arising from 'laws made in the interests of dominant classes'. He believes that it underpins the whole relationship between government and citizen.

Tolstoy, although a political radical who dreamt of the brotherhood of man, held a similar opinion: 'Everywhere and always the laws are enforced by the only means that has compelled, and still compels, some people to obey the will of others, by blows, by deprivation of liberty, and by murder. There can be no other way, (Tolstoy, (ET), p. 111). There is, however, an important difference between Tolstoy and Spencer. While Spencer seeks to minimize the scope of government because of its coercive character, in order to maximize the freedom of the individual to act in his own interests, he does not regard coercion as imparting a morally unfavourable complexion to the practice of government itself: there is, he thinks, no other way in which a society can be organized. Here Tolstoy disagrees: he holds that societies *can* be constituted by relations other than the political, but that in general they *are not* so constituted. And then government can claim no moral advantage over its opponents. The two positions come close together in Marxist theory, where the power of the bourgeois state has to be replaced through the superior power of the workers' state, but only so that the governmental structures of the state itself can eventually be dismantled to create a new kind of society.

To the Hobbesian claim that terrorism represents the 'warre of every man against every man' that is the dreadful alternative to society under a settled government, is opposed the view that society under a settled government is itself disguised *state terrorism*: 'the state consists of those people who have the guns ... and are prepared to use them' (Collins, pp. 351–2). Can such a view be justified?

One's first thought is that it cannot. Surely, in order for the violence of a government to be state terrorism it must itself be in *breach* of the law, in just the same way that anti-state terrorism consists of criminal acts. It is, for example, the activities of 'death squads' who gun down political opponents without affording them due process of law that is paradigmatic of state terrorism. But the claim of governments to moral superiority over terrorists rests precisely on government activity being in *conformity* with the law. There are two replies to this. The radical reply, which we shall examine further shortly, is that all law may be viewed simply as an instrument of oppression, so that adherence to it confers no moral superiority. The modest reply is that certainly *some* laws (e.g. those that permit summary execution, torture or detention without trial of political opponents) are instruments of oppression, and do not wipe out the imputation of state terrorism against these acts. Indeed such laws may well be invalid under international law through the principle of *lex iniusta non est lex* (an unjust law is not a law) so that those who committed these acts might subsequently be tried and punished for their deeds even though the written laws permitted them.

This takes us immediately to the crucial point which brings out how extreme would be the consequences if it turned out that government violence was only state terrorism. It is that acts of state terrorism can not properly be regarded as acts of state, as acts of the government of the state, at all. When government officials act illegally they do not act in their official character, but only as private individuals. And the same holds true of those who commit what are crimes under international law. The paradigm cases of state terrorism are the *private* acts of those who happen to hold government office. The consequence of government violence being no different in kind from anti-state terrorism would therefore be that a putative government so acting lost all claim to be acting as a *government* at all. We would arrive, then, at the conclusion that government personnel are only actors in a power struggle between different sections of the people. Yet it is surely impossible to think of society as constituted by the very hostilities from which, on Hobbes's view, it is our only refuge. For then nothing would distinguish society, for which, Hobbes believes, government is necessary, from the 'disorderly' state of nature with which he contrasts it.

The law and constitution

The consequences of denying the distinction between private acts and acts of state are tellingly illustrated in Joseph Conrad's allegorical story 'An Anarchist'. Escaping from prison, the hero of the title is hailed as their leader by two fellow convicts whom he has coerced into rowing him away from the island.

'We owe you a famous debt of gratitude comrade. You are cut out for a chief.'

'Comrade! Monsieur! Ah what a good word! And they, such men as these two, had made it accursed ... I looked at them and thought that while they lived I could never be free ... 'I must be free', I cried furiously.

'Vive la liberté!' yells that ruffian Mafile. 'Mort aux bourgeois who send us to Cayenne! they shall soon know that we are free.' ... I pulled the trigger of my revolver and shot him ... right through the heart. The other cried out piercingly ... 'Mercy', he whispered, faintly. 'Mercy for me! – Comrade.'

'Ah comrade', I said in a low tone. 'Yes comrade of course. Well then shout Vive l'anarchie.'

He flung up his arms, his face up to the sky and his mouth wide open in a great yell of despair. 'Vive l'anarchie! Vive –'

He collapsed all in a heap, with a bullet through his head. (Conrad, p. 111)

Conrad implies that unless something constrains rulers in what they do then there is no such thing as an act of state, an act of a leader qua leader at all. And he regards this as a *reductio ad absurdum* of the position (which he attributes to anarchists) of those who are opposed to *any* state structures.

Certainly what is required for the notion of acts of state is the idea of a *constitution* within which such acts are performed. A constitution is a set of rules which govern the acts of government officials if these are to count as acts of state. The rules do not however merely *regulate* the actions of the state: they *constitute* certain actions as acts of the state. In the same way, moving the mitre-shaped piece diagonally constitutes moving the bishop in chess, and does not just regulate it: one is no longer playing chess if one moves the bishop some other way. By contrast, the rules which prohibit fouls regulate soccer matches, for soccer is still being played when fouls go undetected (cp. Rawls, (R), pp. 218). If we are to have a coherent conception of acts of state there must therefore be a clear distinction between conforming to constitutional rules and merely seeming to do so. They must exert real constraints on those whose actions are constituted as acts of state by them. It follows that an act cannot become an act of state simply by conforming to the will of a dictator, for this would allow no distinction between an act of state and his private act. If one of the SS chiefs was attempting to report the *constitutional* position in Nazi Germany when he said, 'as long as the police is carrying out the will of the leadership, it is acting legally' (quoted McCoubrey, p. 134) then he must have been wrong. For in those circumstances it would not have been possible for members of the police to act as properly constituted agents of the state at all.

In order to develop a coherent conception of what sort of rules are constitutive of state action we require, I suggest, a notion of the proper *purposes* of the state. Hobbes, we noticed, spoke of defence from 'the invasion of Forraigners, and the injuries of one another' or as a more recent philosopher puts it (reversing the terms) 'the keeping of order and the maintenance of security' (Raphael, p. 46). Order is maintained by enforcing the law, security by military defence. Both are regarded as purely *contingent* methods for achieving the overall aim of protection from two sorts of threat, external and internal. Yet surely this view of the role of law is mistaken. A body which maintained order within a territory by drugging the population would not thereby become its government. By contrast drugging an enemy population might be a possible way for such a body to maintain security. In the former case it could not be acting as a *state*; in the latter case it might. This point has nothing to do with a government's duty to uphold the liberties of citizens and so forth. It is just that it is only as enforcing the *law* that the keeping of *order* counts as an activity of the state.

What is more, the enforcing of the law is, I would suggest, the *only* constitutive purpose of the state. The maintenance of security is simply the safeguarding of territory within which order can be kept by law enforcement. Incursions from without threaten citizens because they cannot be punished under the law: or if the incursions are successful they put the enforcement of the law into other hands. In either case a state would not be able to enforce the law in a land if it could not maintain security. I side then with the eighteenth-century philosopher David Hume in holding that

> We are to look upon all the vast apparatus of our government as having ultimately no other object or purpose but the distribution of justice ... Kings and parliaments, fleets and armies, officers of the court and revenue, ambassadors, ministers and privy-councillors, are all subordinate in their end to this part of administration. (Hume, (E), Part I, Essays)

Now if this is so then we cannot regard law enforcement as *simply* an instrument of oppression by one group of people against another. It is what constitutes their actions as properly *governmental*. And we could go on to say that what holds people together in a society is obedience to the same laws.

So far the notion of constitutionality which we have sketched has been a wide one: constitutional government is government within the law. Yet, as we noticed earlier, governments can pass unjust and oppressive laws which call into question their strictly speaking governmental role itself. This suggests that a narrower notion of constitutionality is needed, in accordance with which only measures which impartially protect citizens will count as laws constitutionally enacted and administered. But as we slip further and further from Hobbes's bare notion of government as a 'common power' so it becomes less and less clear that it is the coercive *force* of government which holds its subjects together in society, rather than its adherence to the principles that govern the application of that force. It is not force which creates society but constraints upon the use of force which preserve it. Subjection to arbitrary force is not society.

The conclusion to draw is surely that it is not shared subordination which constitutes society, but acceptance of the same laws or rules binding upon all. But now it is not clear why this should require coercion rather than common purposes that spring from essentially social motivations. But of this more later.

7.2   Popular Consent

To say that people are held together in society by obedience to the law is still a good way from saying that social relations *between* them are thereby generated, by contrast with the avoidance of social conflict. It is also a good way from saying that being held together in society gives people an *obligation* of obedience to government, as the notion that the social function of government *justifies* its use of force suggest. Hobbes thought of these points as connected and aimed to meet them by a single move. Members of a society, he thought, *agree* to place themselves under a 'Common Power' for mutual protection (Hobbes, chs 17–18). The relations that constitute society are, as a result, of two sorts. Each individual is related to government in virtue of contracting an obligation to obey it, in return for its protection. But each is also related to every other member of society in virtue of contracting this obligation, because he has placed himself under it on the understanding that the other members will do likewise. It is this latter relation which sustains social, as against purely political, bonds. But the relations work together, because unless there is an obligation to government which can be enforced the obligation to one's fellow citizens cannot and people will violate their mutual understanding when it suits them. They honour their obligation to obey government in the face of temptations to break it only because the government punishes disobedience, and this gives them a stronger motive to keep to their agreement with others than to renege on it.

As an account of the basis of social relations this story is, of course, highly speculative. It is risky to argue from the *fact* of political power sufficient to suppress rebellion to the existence of an *obligation* not to rebel. And even if it could be shown that people have consented to obey government, and thereby contracted an obligation to it, there is no reason to think that they have done so through mutual agreement, and thereby contracted an obligation to others. Even if they would not have consented to be governed had others not done likewise no *agreement* with others is implied.

Hobbes's seventeenth-century successor, John Locke, also founded his account of the basis of society on the consent of its members. But, unlike Hobbes, he distinguished their consent 'to join and unite into a community for their comfortable, safe, and peaceable living, one amongst another, in a secure enjoyment of their properties, and a greater security against any that are not of it' (Locke, section 95) from the community's consent to obey a government. The latter is, in his view, not the consent of each individual member, but of the whole community, as determined by a majority of members. The obligation upon each to obey the government derives, he thought, from the fact that in agreeing to enter a community, each gives up his freedom to give or withhold individual consent to what it prescribes as its government. On this view, social relations are not created by the power of government. They antedate it, though no doubt they need government to sustain them. For government has power, within the narrower constitutional limits mentioned in the previous section, because a society already constituted by mutual agreement gives it power. Locke is clear, as Hobbes was not, that power exercised beyond the limits to which society would consent is not, properly speaking, the power of government.

We shall look, in the next section, at the contrasting conception of society which Locke employs. Now we need to look at the notion, shared in different forms by Hobbes and Locke, that it is *consent* which justifies government in its exercise of power and which creates an obligation to obey the law. For mutual consent to the same government would seem to be some evidence of membership of the same society. The problem is to explain why a government, a body which wields the power needed to enforce the law, should be accorded the right to do so. It is the problem of how to show that the political order might match the social order, so that members of a society might owe an obligation of loyalty to the government which regulates their social life. The difficulty in knowing how to solve this problem in contemporary societies is sometimes known as 'the legitimation crisis' (see Habermas, (LC)).

Hobbes himself held that, broadly speaking, *any* government is an overwhelming advantage to its citizens, who are therefore quite unjustified in trying to overthrow it by force. But most theorists who adopt a largely Hobbesian view of the political character of society would dissent from this. Some citizens may be so disadvantaged by a particular system of government as to be better off without it, in which case a more satisfactory one might arise. On this view arguments against violent opposition will be available only in a *democratic* state for in a democracy, it is declared, there is agreement between citizens to the government. After all the government is elected by them. The government of a democratic state is responsive to the claims of different interest groups, which others are not. Any other kind of state, then, is potentially unstable and lacks the degree of social cohesion that adherence to democratically agreed laws can provide. It is in this way that the relations that constitute a society can be forged according to democratic theory.

If this is really so (and it is an empirical question whether it is), then a challenge to democratic institutions really is a threat to orderly society; it threatens its continued existence. Violent opposition to a democratic government must, then, be treated as a criminal offence – albeit politically motivated – for otherwise the government will not be exercising its responsibility to its electors to enforce the law. And in a democratic state the law does not just provide a *tactic* for controlling opposition. It expresses the mutually agreed rules that bind members of the society together and which must, therefore, be impartially applied to them. If it is not, then some are already being regarded as no longer members of society. As the nineteenth-century utilitarian Jeremy Bentham said of rebellion:

> When the persons by whom it is perpetrated are of such force as to bid defiance to the ordinary efforts of justice, they loosen themselves from their original denomination in proportion as they increase in force, till at length they are looked upon as being no longer members of the state, but as standing altogether upon a footing with external adversaries. (Bentham, p. 349)

By this time then society, as it was, has broken down.

Democratic theory offers an attractive supplement to the Hobbesian view of how society is constituted politically. Where there is democracy

there does appear to be evidence of agreement between people to conform to common laws and hence to be members of the same society.
That seems to justify a 'war against terrorism' and the like on society's
behalf. But appearances can be deceptive. Democratic theory has a fatal
flaw. For there are some matters which democratic processes cannot
decide.

Paramount among these is the question of *who* the members of a
given state – and hence a society – should be. For a majority vote
obviously cannot decide *who* shall vote to decide *this* issue. Yet who
shall vote is, in democratic theory, precisely the question of who the
members of the state should be (allowing for complications concerning
children and others deemed ineligible to vote). Where there is a dispute
over this – as over the extent of the state of Ireland, for example – there
will also be no agreement on who shall vote to resolve it. It is evident
that the widespread connection between terrorism and movements of
national secession or unification can be explained by this limitation on
the scope of democratic processes. For on this kind of question the
democrat's arguments against violent opposition fall away. The reason is
that democratic processes cannot decide *what* group of people shall
form a society. Over the question whether we wish to be formed into
just this society, rather than some other, democratic institutions can
provide no evidence of consent.

Furthermore, although a state needs to secure its territories in order
to carry out its constitutive purpose of enforcing of the law, there is no
evident reason why it should secure just *these* territories, with their
population, rather than some others. The state's constitutive purpose
provides no justification for a state to claim that it must maintain its
existing borders, or any others. The maintenance of a particular state's
structure, and hence on the Hobbesian view, a particular society, is, as
perhaps Hobbes himself recognized, a product not of agreement, but of
enmity and war. The *particular* societies that there are exist, under their
governments, until they come peaceably or violently apart, but no
argument can be adduced from their democratic organization to dis-
suade those who seek to be in different social relations from violence to
that end. If communities exist by the mutual consent of their members,
it is not in democratic structures that this consent consists.

7.3   *Community and Association*

We need to return now to consider the alternative to Hobbes's view that
societies only exist by permission – perhaps we should rather say, by

order – of governments. The example he gives of 'the state of nature', the condition of the woodland Indians of his day such as the Iroquois, proved an ironic choice. For over two centuries later Friedrich Engels took the Iroquois as an instance of an orderly society which nevertheless lacked coercive government: 'No nobles, no gendarmes or police, no nobles, kings, regents, prefects, or judges, no prisons, no law suits ... all are equal and free – the women included,' he enthused (Engels, ch. 3). Hobbes and Engels were in fact both wrong about the Iroquois. They had a social organization which, while geared to tribal warfare, was maintained, not spontaneously, but through a rigidly stratified matriarchy (cp. Farb, ch. 7). Yet Engels had a better grasp of the realities of social anthropology than did Hobbes. For there certainly are – or at least have been – societies without coercive governments. The Nuer people of the Sudan are an example, who, although they have 'the principle that certain actions are offences, and that a person who has suffered an offence is entitled to redress', have no central government to enforce it (Mair, (PG), p. 36); hence they fall to fighting, not to secure their interests, as Hobbes would think, but to protect their rights, no clear notion of which exists outside society.

These facts present us with the possibility that Hobbes's theory is upside down; that far from human societies being formed by the strong hand of government, government arises from societies formed from quite other relations.

This, as we have seen, is the view that John Locke held. While Hobbes thought that the cessation of government spelt the end of society Locke quite specifically denies this.

> He that will with any clearness speak of the dissolution of government, ought in the first place to distinguish between the dissolution of the society and the dissolution of the government. That which makes the community, and brings men out of the state of nature into one polite society, is the agreement which every one has with the rest to incorporate and act as one body, and to be one distinct commonwealth. The usual, and almost the only way whereby the union is dissolved, is the inroad of foreign force making a conquest upon them. (Locke, section 211)

In other cases, he says:

> ... When the government is dissolved, the people are at liberty to provide for themselves by erecting a new legislative ... For the society can never, by the fault of another, lose the native and original right it has to preserve itself, which can only be done by a settled legislative and a fair and impartial execution of the laws made by it. (Locke, section 220)

Indeed if laws to protect citizens are not administered, Locke holds that society is justified in overturning the government and replacing it.

We can see the alternatives most sharply by looking at two contrasting conceptions of the law. On the Hobbesian view which we have been considering, laws are *commands* of the government to its citizens backed by threats of enforcement through the power of the state. On this account (sometimes referred to as *legal positivism*), laws are designed to maintain order, that is, to prevent the conflicts that arise from competition between individuals. Their justification therefore lies in the efficiency with which they perform this task. We can compare the command theory of law with what we might call the *normative* one (often rather misleadingly known as *legal naturalism*). The normative theory locates the ultimate authority of the law not in a government's power to enforce it, but in its expression of essentially moral principles, principles as to how to live together well. In ideal circumstances social life would be guided by these principles without requiring the sanctions available to a coercive government. Only in specific circumstances is the power of government required to enforce the law, and then it acts on behalf of society, for breaches of the law are offences against society which is constituted by mutual adherence to the principles that the law expresses.

The normative conception of law allows that the laws imposed by government may not properly reflect the principles accepted in society. (Hence the suggestion that 'unjust law is not law' alluded to earlier.) An interesting example of such a judgement about the law is a central theme of Mrs Gaskell's nineteenth-century novel *Sylvia's Lovers*, set in north-eastern England during the Napoleonic wars. When the press-gang seizes sailors, who have just returned home after many months on the whaling ships, for service in the navy they are forcibly freed by a mob. The ringleader is hanged, but he says,

> 'a'm noane sorry for what a did, an'a'd do it again toneet if need were . . .
> so theere's for thee. Thou may tell t'justices fra'me that a reckon a did
> righter nor them, as letten poor fellys be carried off i't'very middle
> o't'town they're called justices for.' (Gaskell, ch. 24)

The state's commands are not here viewed as safeguarding society, even in time of war, but as a possible threat to ordinary social life.

We see, then, immediately that the normative theory of law implies a quite different account of what constitutes society. It is again adherence to the law, but adherence which springs not from fear of sanctions but from a view of the law as, in the main, determining how it is good to live with others. The conception of society involved here is, we can say, *communitarian*. It views societies as communities, or groups of people living a common life together. What is important about this account lies in its contrast with the Hobbesian one. There the *purpose* of coming together into a society under one government is to prevent conflict: that is what laws are for. In the communitarian conception there is no clear purpose in social organization, any more than there is in living itself. The prevention of conflict is, of course, necessary for living together, but this is not a separate purpose which they subserve, since what counts as unacceptable conflict can only be identified in terms of the breaking of these rules.

The contrast between the communitarian and Hobbesian conceptions of society exemplifies a distinction drawn by the late nineteenth- ... and early twentieth-century sociologist Ferdinand Toennies. Toennies distinguishes community (Gemeinschaft) from association (Gesellschaft) (Toennies, p. 131ff.). In Toennies's sense a community is a social group not formed for any definite purpose or deliberately organized but valued for its own sake. Toennies thought of families, groups of friends and so forth as communities: we shall restrict the term to groups whose members have a less limited range of common concerns, like traditional villages or perhaps whole societies. By contrast with communities are associations, which are formed for an explicit purpose and organized to attain it, such as trade unions or political parties. The state on the Hobbesian view clearly counts as an association in Toennies's sense. For it has a purpose – the prevention of conflict – and a definite organization to attain it – its law enforcement structures and so forth. But the Hobbesian conception of society allows us to draw no sharp distinction between society and the state, for without the state there would be no society, only an aggregate of individuals.

In all *actual* cases, however, associations *presuppose* communities. There can be no question of people identifying specific purposes and organizing to achieve them unless they already know what it is to live together socially. Hobbes's notion of society itself as the product of an association is self-defeatingly over-ambitious. With it too must go his notion of individuals as essentially non-social. Yet though his picture of competing individuals is not an empirically well-supported one, it is forced on us if we can only think of the state as an association whose purpose is to prevent conflict between them. It is, one might say, a presupposition of forming an association with this purpose that people are to be thought of in this way. If that is what the modern state is like – and the issue is arguable – then far from establishing social relations it may be thought to have a tendency to undermine them, since by substituting motives to further *individual* interests without attracting undesirable consequences it may obscure a concern as to how to live well *together*. The mechanism for such a process would of course involve the dissemination of the Hobbesian view of the individual in society as an *ideological* one, which, if the theory of ideology is correct, would serve the interests and justify the practice of those who benefit from and who can maintain the power of the modern state.

The Hobbesian model of society, however, is avoidable. And it is avoidable, the communitarian argues, without cost to our ordinary conception of ourselves as standing in social relations to others. The communitarian conception regards these relations as essentially reciprocal relations springing from a recognition that we do live together with others and have a large range of common interests in consequence. We have common interests in maintaining or improving in multifarious ways our conditions of life, which are threatened by shared dangers and afflictions; we have common interests in meeting together and forming personal relationships; we have common interests in preserving or changing large-scale organizations, such as the state. This last conflict prevention interest has no precedence over the others. A network of *different* social relations is generated by the reciprocal pursuit of them. Each common interest links us to different groups of people. Perhaps it is only the last – the relation in which we stand to others as fellow citizens – that relates us, however abstractedly, to *all* members of our political community. But that is no reason to give it priority as *the* relation which constitutes us as members of the same *society*, in so far as we can distinguish political from social groupings. Indeed, as we shall see, it need not correspond to the network of relationships which does.

The network of relationships which constitutes a society is characterized by the fact that the parties to particular social relations are interchangeable: were others from the society to occupy their places the same social relations would bind them. The reason for this is that each member of society accepts the same rules for performing their parts and expects others to do likewise. It is this which makes possible the mutual trust and commitment in the pursuit of common purposes which binds members of the same society together. This is not to say that what makes people members of the same society is that they have a sense of being so (*pace* Mabbott, p. 82). That would indeed be circular. But nor is it to say only that they are more similar in the way they live than members of other societies. For they must have a sense of this similarity, not only as a fact about them, but as something expected of them. And this must be the basis of a shared view not just of how they do live together, but of how it is good to live.

The communitarian conception allows no essential connection between the identity of a society and its separate statehood. The same society could fall under several states or one state could control several distinct societies. But, unlike the Hobbesian conception, even when that is amplified by democratic theory, the communitarian conception does provide a rationale for separate statehood. For *independent* government is required to ensure that the laws applied to a society reflect the rules regulating its social relationships and not alien rules. And *self*-government is needed to prevent one group which controls the government benefiting at the expense of society as a whole, by enforcing laws otherwise than to reflect those rules. Rebellions, terrorism and other acts against the state commonly proceed from the conviction that a certain society is not appropriately governed. Far from necessarily threatening the existence of the society they may, however misguidedly, set out to preserve it.

The communitarian conception of society may seem a conservative one, tying the laws of the state to the existing customs of its citizens and not allowing for change or cultural diversity. I do not see that these are necessary consequences of accepting it; for what social rules there are will change as different common purposes present themselves and different people are brought together to pursue them. And how these rules should be reflected in the laws of the state will be a matter for those pursuing these purposes collectively to determine.

Yet there is of course an enormous political divide here between those who think of the state as properly under the control of the collectivity – of society as a whole – and those who think of it as responding only to the expression of individual interests. The existence of democratic institutions can obscure this divide, since as Rousseau noted (see above 6.3), there is still the question of how one should vote in a democracy – whether as an individual with a variety of interests and concerns, or simply as a member of the state. Such questions are political: they concern what one takes the *right* relation between the state and society to be. Evidently this will be influenced by one's view of what society *is*. But here sharp distinctions between what is and what ought to be are elusive. For what a given society is like – what sorts of social relations characterize it – is influenced by the conception that its members have of it and that is shaped by what they want and expect it to be.

In the final chapter we shall look at some of the ways in which our relationships might be criticized or changed.

Further reading

Hobbes's *Leviathan*, of course, especially chapters 13–21. The even more radical view of the state as monopolizing violence has been popular amongst sociologists since Max Weber: see Antony Giddens's *The Nation-State and Violence*. Harry Beran's *The Consent Theory of Political Obligation* gives a modern defence of a traditional view. But how should separatist claims be treated and what other challenges to a democratic state's claim to legitimacy might there be (e.g. revolutionary ones)?

A version of the communitarian theory has recently been defended as a basis for democratic institutions in Carol Gould's *Rethinking Democracy*, chapter 2. What arguments might there be for preferring it to individualism as a view of what our political relations *should* be?

8

Family Matters

8.1 Nostalgia or Utopia?

We enter the world already cocooned in a web of relationships. We grow up in them and come to accept them – the family or some surrogate for it, almost everywhere – as the norm. It is only much later that we can ask whether we are right to do so. For even if there is no practical possibility of changing our own individual relationships there is a question of whether they are ones we have a good reason for participating in, or whether there might be other better relationships which we could value more highly, so that we could collectively change our social relationships. And in asking this question we must wonder whether our answers are themselves determined by what we have been brought up to value in the relationships we do find ourselves in, and to what extent we can break away from them.

Two pictures of human relationships commonly compete for our approval. And they compete particularly, perhaps, when we think about relations within the family. One is a *nostalgic* picture, of relationships having once been more as they ought to be, when familial roles were accepted unquestioningly and close family bonds were forged by un-reflective feeling. Modern *mores* distort and corrupt social lives that would otherwise be well spent. The other is a *Utopian* picture, of relationships as they have never been but ought to be, in which familial roles are redefined and our attachments and sympathies to others are determined by a rational assessment of our respective needs. Traditional customs and attachments obstruct the development of social lives that might otherwise be satisfied. The two pictures are characteristically associated with two views concerning the plasticity of human relationships. According to the nostalgic picture our most basic relationships are *given*, and, while not necessarily unchanging, not directly change-able at will. According to its Utopian rival they are *fashioned* to suit specific human needs in particular circumstances, and can be refashioned if they cease to do so.

There is a natural connection between being attracted to the nostalgic picture and accepting a view of our more basic relationships as *communal* in Toennies's sense: as relationships we enter without explicit ends in view, though with a sense of their value. And there is a similar connec-tion between the Utopian picture and an *associational* view of them: in which we think of relationships as having definite purposes for which we enter them. Yet I do not believe that a communal view commits its supporters to nostalgia. It permits criticism and rational change, while putting obstacles in the way of some Utopian excesses. One reason for doubting the possibility of rational change stems from confusing rela-tionships that are *given*, which we find ourselves involved in without any sense of their answering to antecedently identified purposes, with ones that are *natural*, which we are involved in by virtue of facts about our natural history. If basic human relationships were natural (and we have argued in chapter 2 against accepting this account of them) then indeed it is hard to see how they could be criticized and changed. But those that are given have this role only because of their centrality and inescapability in a certain society: in different societies different rela-tionships may occupy this place. Change may be possible, not the better to serve specific purposes, but to correct their moral drawbacks.

Let us turn, then, to consider criticisms of the kinds of relationship we may find ourselves in. We have already noted (in chapter 6) one kind of criticism that might be made about relationships characterized by collective reciprocity, namely that they impair individual autonomy. Indeed this kind of criticism can be made more generally of any rela-tionship in which we simply find ourselves conforming to norms with-out any sense of their answering to our purposes. So what if we judge that they are not? Well, the fact that I simply find myself in a rela-tionship does not imply that I am not free to leave it, difficult as this may be in practice. There is no necessary connection between the givenness of a relationship and its involuntariness. I cannot choose no longer to be someone's son or father; but I can generally choose whether to play the expected roles that go with these relationships. There may be no alternative ways to play these roles available, so that in this sense they are inescapable. But this poses a threat to my autonomy – rather than just to my social life – only if a *possible* form of rela-tionship, which does answer to my purposes, is one I am somehow *prevented* from engaging in.

This presupposes, however, that we can coherently value what is offered by the relationships in which we find ourselves, while escaping the constraints they impose upon us. Yet there are narrow limits upon the extent to which individuals can, in principle, redesign their relationships to suit their particular purposes. It is, for example, outlandish to suppose that relationships characterized by mutual *feeling* can be *willed* into existence. What we may say about the relationships which Utopians contrive – like 'free love' – is that they are sentimental: the feelings they involve lack seriousness, however well-meaning their participants. And that is because it is a criterion of the depth of social feelings, like love, for instance, that they do bind us to others in ways above and beyond what, were we not affected by them, we would will. The alternative to accepting close relationships as given rather than manufactured is not a life of feeling but of manufactured feeling, which is no kind of genuine feeling (though the value of feeling itself can, as we shall shortly see, be questioned). The givenness of such relationships is, then, a necessary condition upon the scope of our autonomy.

A distinct kind of criticism of existing familial relations is that they are dysfunctional: that, far from conducing to human welfare, they militate against it in a variety of ways. The sexually exclusive couple, it may be said, breeds frustration and resentment. Nor is it the optimal arrangement for sexual relations within a society, since many members will be unable to find anyone with whom they can live on these terms (Gregory, pp. 265–7). The couple with children devotes more time and concern to them than is reasonable, and, what is more, competes with others for resources to expend upon them, subverting the solidarity of society. These criticisms are criticisms from considerations of *utility*.

Some of them struck Plato when in the *Republic* he devised an ideal society. (Sir Thomas More's sixteenth-century fable partly modelled on the *Republic* gives us the name *Utopia*.) In Plato's ideal society 'our men and women guardians [who constitute the ruling class] should be forbidden by law to live together in separate households, and wives should be held in common by all; and similarly children should be held in common, and no parent should know his child, or child his parent' (marginal, p. 457). The resulting society will look bleak to most of us, though some of its ideas have appealed to others, for example to the early kibbutz movement in Israel.

Yet two points need making about this, construed as a criticism of existing family relationships. First, it is in fact an attack on certain *social institutions*, not the relationships which lie behind them. It suggests an end to *monogamous marriage* and to *parental responsibility* which are institutions enshrined in law. Old-style relationships could no doubt survive their dismantling. Plato, however, believes that their replacement by different institutions will generate new relationships. He does not, then, assume that relationships can be altered at will *directly*. Rather the utility of relationships is to be enhanced by creating institutions which function more satisfactorily.

The second point is that Plato covertly accepts that it is on relationships that are already given that such new relationships will need to be modelled. What looks to us like the destruction of the family is presented by him as its extension.

> 'What about our Guardians? Could any of them seriously say he had nothing to do with his fellows?'
>
> 'Certainly not ... for he is bound to regard any of them he meets as related to him, as brother or sister, father or mother, son or daughter, grandparent or grandchild.'
>
> 'You are quite right. And here is a further point. They won't be allowed to treat these relationships as merely nominal, but will be required to behave accordingly. They will be expected to show their fathers all the customary honour, love and obedience.' (Plato, (R), marginal p. 463)

Notice that the same *feelings* – like love – as are found in existing families, are expected to bind the guardians together. For the bonds created by these feelings create a sense of unity and solidarity which is to be valued. It is only that the relationship thereby forged needs to be widened to embrace a whole community (or at least its ruling class; Plato is unclear on this), if its unity is not be undermined by narrower ties. Whether this wider bond might come about may be doubted, as it was by Aristotle.

> In a state having women and children in common, love will be diluted: and the father will not say 'my son', or the son 'my father'. As a little sweet wine mingled with a great deal of water is imperceptible in the mixture, so in this sort of community the idea of a relationship which is based upon these names will be lost. (Aristotle, (P), 4.1262)

The disagreement here is not as to the *value* of this kind of relationship – only as to its possible scope. And this is common to many criticisms of relationships as dysfunctional. It is not the nature of the relationships themselves that is criticized, but the pattern of these relationships in society. But when we consider recommendations for change we need also to think of what resulting patterns of relationships would be available to individuals (cp. Sidgwick, p. 359). The range of relationships with different degrees of intimacy and of closeness locate individuals in relation to others in a way that it is not easy for us as participants to grasp explicitly, though this range is reflected in clear differences of feeling between people. But we are certainly not entitled, as Aristotle saw, to assume that the *same* emotions could survive radical changes in the patterns of relationships available to us.

A third, and perhaps the most radical, criticism of existing relationships derives however from questioning the value of these social emotions themselves. They lead, it is suggested, to partiality in our actions towards others, which cannot be justified by any differences in their claims upon us. Our emotions create unfairness and, more generally, irrationality. We have already seen (4.2) a version of this kind of criticism in Plato's advice to the lover in the *Symposium* to 'abate his violent love of the one', when he sees that 'the beauty of one form is akin to the beauty of another'. If he does not, the lover's partiality to the beloved will not be due to any relevant point of difference between him and others. By implication it will just be an emotion which assails him, not a rationally grounded preference.

A further, and perhaps more persuasive, version of the criticism is to be found in the ethical system of the great eighteenth-century philosopher Immanuel Kant. Kant distinguishes 'practical' from 'pathological' love. The former resides 'in the will and not in the propensions of feeling, in principles of action and not of melting compassion; and it is this practical love alone which can be an object of command' (Kant, p. 67). Practical love is, in other words, a disposition to act benevolently to those who are in need, irrespective of any relationship we may have towards them that is founded on feeling. Pathological love by contrast is an 'inclination' which motivates people to help others, but is felt towards some of them and not towards all, at some times and not always. But because acts of pathological love stem from feelings which simply come over us, rather than from a rational appreciation of what it is right to do, they lack, in Kant's view, any of the ethical merit that acts of practical love possess (cp. Kierkegaard, pp. 94–6).

On this sort of view, any of our existing relationships which involve different degrees of concern for others are suspect. A more rational society would be one where we were not prey to the affections which generate such partiality. We shall look at the conception of emotion involved here in the next section. It is worth remarking, however (cp. Blum, ch. 3), that the notion of *complete* impartiality between competing claims upon us is one that has its source in situations where the person from whom it is expected – a judge or a social security benefit assessor, for example – is meant to stand in *no* relevant relationship to those whose claims he arbitrates upon. It is, therefore, hard to see how it could be a model for a new kind of *relationship* to others.

In other situations our conception of what is partial, of what discriminates unfairly and of what is impartial derives from our understanding of what is due to some, to members of our family say, and not to others, by contrast with what we owe to all. Yet our understanding of this is itself open to criticism: perhaps some kinds of help offered to one's children, like an expensive private education, for example, *are* unfair. Others evidently are not: no one could argue that it was unfair to unloved children to lavish love on one's own. But these kinds of criticism cannot derive from an absolutely *general* view about how all relationships ought to be. Rather, they derive from a grasp of what is worthwhile in the sort of relationship in which we find ourselves and of how to balance the demands of different ones. Wanting what is best for our children is an expression of parental love if it manifests concern for their welfare, but not if it demonstrates vicarious ambition, since this undermines concern for them as they are, rather than as *we* would want them to be. A grasp of what values the relationship aims at is what provides the material for criticism of some of its forms. And again a grasp of the kind of care adults owe to other children in the community as against their own is needed to assess current practice. A further example of this general pattern of criticizing relationships from within a practice was given in discussing the feminist critique of love (above, 3.4). Uncritical nostalgia is not forced on us by these facts, far from it. Yet in the light of them Utopia, which prescinds from all existing relationships, is literally unthinkable.

8.2 *Passion and Participation*

Our relationships are founded upon emotion, and the closer the relationships the more intense those emotions are. It is not just that emotions accompany them. We cannot conceive of something being what we would want to call 'love' or 'friendship' or 'loyalty', unless the actions arising from it were due to the emotions it involved. But if these emotions are thought of as simply assailing us – as Kant, for example, thinks of them – then it seems that we are drawn blindly by them into relationships for which we may be able to give no reason and in which, even if we can give a reason, reason is not the operative force.

The picture is a familiar, and a romantic, one. It is analogous to the picture of desires as blind forces which we looked at and rejected in chapter 2. Indeed it is a version of this picture, for emotions involve desires and aversions, which is why they can move us to act. And yet this picture of the emotions in our relationships may seem a persuasive one. For is it not the case that in relationships we *are* often overcome by passion and act contrary to our better judgement? While our desires generally may be subject to rational scrutiny and possible revision, are our emotions not outside of such control? True, we can sometimes 'control our feelings'; but this is to say that we control their *expression*, rather than restrain the impulses that they involve. And at other times we cannot even control that: we blush or cry or shout involuntarily. And the activities fundamental to our relationships – a kiss, an exchange of smiles, working in unison – often seem to have this character, arising involuntarily from mutual feeling. How then can the kinds of relationship we have be answerable to reasons?

There is a web of confusion here which it is hard to disentangle. First, we need to rid ourselves of the idea that emotions simply assail us in the way that sensations like pains or itches do. The assumption that they do stems from the fact that emotions often involve sensations which do so assail us – tremors of love, a warm glow of friendship and so forth. It is characteristically such sensations which give rise to the involuntary behaviour that expresses social emotions, just as pains produce involuntary reactions that express distress. But, and this is the second point, emotions arise from *thoughts* about the world. I think of her as a possible partner and am filled with love. I recognize him as my child and am overcome with concern. The sensations and bodily reactions are concomitants of these thoughts. For emotions are 'intentional' states, in the technical, philosophical sense of this word. That is to say, they are *directed* at objects, real or imaginary, which are given in thought. I cannot feel just love: it must be love *for* someone, and for them in some possible relationship to me. I am concerned *about* something befalling someone, in the light of what I, in my relationship to them, might do to help. And the thoughts that give rise to emotions may be sensible or wild. So, though in practice I may not always be able to ensure that they are sensible, in principle I can bring reason to bear on them, and hence on the emotions themselves.

Thirdly however, emotions involve an *evaluation* of actions and events involving their objects. I think of her as good to be with, of him as to be helped and comforted. My feelings go out to those with whom I have relationships in my inclinations to such actions, or in my reactions to events affecting them. But these inclinations or reactions are ones that involve evaluations of the actions and events as desirable or otherwise.

So, here again, reasons can and should be brought to bear in assessing the apparent desirability of our social actions, or of the events that trigger them. Yet, fourthly, the apparent desirability of our social activities is not generally or necessarily the result of *judgements* as to their value; and this is no doubt why it can seem to lie beyond the scope of rational scrutiny and hence outside our control. But this conclusion is misguided. We can assess the strength and seriousness of our inclinations, their coherence with or discontinuity from others, their capacity to unlock latent feelings or their merely specious appeal, in a word, the extent to which we should be guided by them, without first arriving at judgements as to the value of the actions to which they lead. Indeed it is hard to see how such judgements, divorced from feeling, *could* bring us to decide the direction of our social acts. These ought to be determined, surely, by how much we should be *affected* by the situation of others. Yet there is no reason to think that this can be assessed other than by the reflective re-ordering of our existing *emotions*. The Kantian notion that the process can be by-passed by appeal to judgements which owe nothing to emotions has little to recommend it once its false view of feeling has been rejected.

The way is open to seeing relationships, with their different and variously *felt* demands, as the very place where the value of meeting the claims of others is disclosed to us. Far from standing in the way of a clear view of their value, social emotions like love, friendship, fraternity or communal sympathy, *present* the meeting of these claims as valuable and thereby motivating, in a way that mere judgements of value could not. We are *affected* by the other's distress and moved to comfort them. We are *thrilled* by their success and want to share it. We *feel* solidarity with them and are *determined* to give our support. These are emotions leading to actions proper to the situations in which we find ourselves through participating in relationships. And they are necessary to our responding appropriately to them. Social emotions, we might say, *are* a participant's view of the value of the activities to which they lead. If we try to stay outside the participant's standpoint we cannot expect to find in judgements about the situations of others anything that can motivate us to react to them as we do. Yet this is not because such judgements would incline us to act differently – more fairly, say – but because they would not incline us to particular acts at all. Of course we can act generously to those we do not know, but this is not from a detached and passionless apprehension of their needs. It is from imaginatively repositioning ourselves in relation to them, which will be impossible were our existing position vis-à-vis some others – the members of our own family, say – not one of passionate involvement.

8.3 *Relativities*

I have suggested that we can criticize our existing relationships only from a position inside of them, and that consequently Utopian transformations are impossible if they seek to identify values that relationships might serve independently of a recognition of their current ends.

Yet this suggests a very radical doubt. Suppose we *can* only criticize our existing relationships from within because there is no way of grasping their value from a position outside of them. Then what *counts* as worthwhile would be relative to societies with particular patterns of relationships. Why should we suppose that our *own* are objectively worthwhile, since quite *other* sorts of relationships will, in the societies in which they occur, seem similarly worthwhile to their participants? But we cannot think of theirs as worthwhile, nor can they think this of ours. In that case it appears that the value we attribute to our relationships is only a reflection of the fact that we are brought up to participate in them, rather than something which provides a justification for participation. Criticism of relationships can effect only change, not, in any objective sense, improvement.

This position constitutes *cultural relativism* with respect to social values. It takes its starting point from the enormous range of relationships that anthropologists have discovered. Thus one sociologist comments on the apparent inevitability of a young American's values as follows:

> We know very well that having many wives or being one of many husbands is not a betrayal of humanity in any biological sense, or even of virility. And since it is biologically possible for Arabs to have the one and for Tibetans to be the other, it must also ·be biologically possible for our young man. Indeed, we know that if the latter had been snatched out of his cradle and shipped to the right alien shores at an early enough age, he would not have grown up to be the red-blooded and more than slightly sentimental all-American boy ... but would have developed into a lusty polygamist in Arabia or a contented multiple husband in Tibet. That is, he is deceiving himself (or, more accurately, being deceived by society) when he looks upon his course of action in this matter as inevitable. This means that every institutional structure must depend on deception and all existence in society carries with it an element of bad faith. (Berger, pp. 106–7)

The implication here is that the sense of inescapability in our relationships, which stems from the assumption that they are justified by their value, is a deception perpetrated upon the members of society to induce them to accept the existing order. Other patterns would be equally possible, but would have to be justified by different values, values in which 'red-bloodedness' and 'sentimentality' have no place. (Notice however, that, despite himself, the author of this paradoxically ethnocentric passage cannot resist interpreting polygamy and polyandry as potentially worthwhile in terms of Western notions of 'lustiness' and 'contentment'.)

If cultural relativism is true, then the kind of understanding we can acquire of our relationships will simply be to grasp the values that we attribute to them. But this will in no way explain why we *should* desire them; it will only show what sort of coherence there is in the fact that we *do* desire them. We will be left with the brute fact that we desire what we have been brought up to think of as desirable, and this will differ from one society to another.

The trouble with cultural relativism about social values, however, is that it *assumes* that the diversity of social practices makes mutual understanding impossible. Such an assumption cannot be justified by the evidence which anthropologists adduce. For, it will be replied, there is another possibility here: the circumstances of another society may be so different from our own that we cannot conceive what it would be like to live and act as they do (cp. Putnam, p. 161). In that case we shall not grasp what value they find in their distinctive relationships. But the reason for this need not be that their values are *different* from our own, rather than that we cannot see how they are to be realized in such very different relationships. We need not, for example, doubt that it is *love* that is shown by a woman who urges her husband to take additional wives in an Islamic society. But we may not be able to see this course of action as desirable as an expression of love, and hence not grasp how social institutions in which it is so regarded can realize the value that attaches to love. Our inability here need not be different in kind from our inability to make sense of the actions of members of our own society, through not being able to put ourselves in their very different situations.

What we fail to grasp here seems very different from what we feel we cannot comprehend in learning that the female praying mantis commonly eats the male while it is mating with her. But then we do not even know how to *start* trying to understand it, since nothing can count as imagining oneself in the situation of the praying mantis. This is not the case with imagining oneself in a different cultural setting; for, although no doubt there are extreme difficulties and dangers here (see the discussion of *The American* in chapter 5.3), one can seek parallels in one's culture as a clue to discovering how some practice may be valued in another. We can see how this might be done by cosidering an example cited by the philosopher of social science Peter Winch in 'Understanding a Primitive Society'. At first it may seem incomprehensible that aboriginals should treat a stick which they carry with them as their soul and view its loss as a sort of death. But Winch reminds us of our own attitude to the carrying of a locket which symbolizes our beloved, and of our regret at its loss. There can be no assurance that we will be able to understand the practices of others in this way. Winch's suggestion is, however, that there is no other way, and there is no reason to think that this way is foredoomed to failure.

This stems from the fact that, unlike the praying mantis, the member of an alien society is thought of as acting for a reason, doing something they see as desirable. Yet what we can count as acting for a reason cannot be *in principle* opaque to us. We may not in practice be able to grasp another's reasons, but if we could not in principle grasp how they can see something as desirable then we would have no reason to accept that it was as something desirable that they pursued it. It would be just as if we were told that a mathematical calculation was in principle beyond our grasp: then we would have no reason to think of it as a *calculation*, whose aim is to get the *right* answer.

The conclusions of Winch and other philosophers who think that we can only understand other cultures from the standpoint of our own have been attacked as conservative. The contemporary German philosopher Hans Georg Gadamer, for example, who in *Truth and Method* describes this process as a 'fusion of horizons', our own and that of the culture we seek to understand, has been criticized on these grounds by Jurgen Habermas in his review of Gadamer's book (Habermas (R)). Habermas believes that the consensus of values within a culture must be open to criticism on rational grounds, which can in principle be applied to *any* value system. But how might such rational grounds for comprehensive criticism be identified? Habermas's answer is to postulate an 'ideal speech situation'. In this situation the participants are to be motivated solely by the desire to come to an agreement on some subject, for example what social practice would best allow for some activity. The participants must withhold consideration of their own individual interests, rather as in Rousseau's conception of the 'general will'; they must also be prepared to jettison their pre-existing values. In this situation they will all participate on an equal footing and supposedly reach a rational consensus. Habermas supposes that this consensus will tend towards truth, and to justice and freedom in practical agreements. To the extent to which existing social practices deviate from such norms, that is because of the repression of tendencies towards these ends which results from existing power relations. For in so far as our own current norms do so deviate, they simply serve to 'stabilize relations of force' (Habermas, (LC), p. 111).

There is an affinity between Habermas's attempt to find extra-cultural norms and that of the American philosopher John Rawls (see Rawls, (J), part I). Rawls suggests that if we want to discover what really is a just society we put ourselves in the 'original position' of ignorance as to our eventual place in the social order and decide, from that standpoint, what sort of society we should prefer. Existing power relations are thus neutralized in the resulting consensus which maximizes freedom and secures equality unless inequalities benefit the disadvantaged.

Similar criticisms can be mounted against both views. In the first place their postulate of people coming together to decide on their social practices implicitly assumes an associational model, in Toennies's sense, of the resulting relationships. But then no room will have been allowed for the values of communal relationships. Secondly and connectedly, a conception of the optimal relationships as those that best serve individual interests seems also to be assumed in the sort of calculation it is thought that the participants will make. But thirdly, there is no reason to think that when *we* consider what our reactions in the 'ideal speech situation' or 'original position' would be we are doing anything other than import into it our own culturally inherited values. And fourthly, what will strike us as reasonable in taking *these* situations as ones in which we can best determine our social practices surely can only be that these situations strike us as free, fair and conducive to truth. This is surely because they approximate to the ones we favour highly in our own society. Ironically perhaps, these seem to be the collective decision-making situations of traditional communal relations.

I conclude, therefore, that we have no choice but to think about alternatives to our relationships in the light of values we acquire within them. This in no way militates against, indeed it is a condition of, criticism of our relationships. What is more, there is no reason to suppose that it denies us access to possible values. But if it does not, this is not because those values can be explained in terms of facts about human nature or the results of individual choice exercised in optimal conditions. To suppose that they must be is to confuse values that are *definable*, in the sense that they can be explained to us in the light of what we already value, with those that are *instrumental*, that merely conduce to further values. But the fact that we value certain kinds of relationship *for their own sake* does not imply that we cannot *clarify* the sort of value that they have. If it did, the preceding discussions would have been foredoomed to failure.

It would be satisfying to conclude with some suggestions for the reform of our relationships. But this would run counter to the drift of this chapter. Only the participants in them can negotiate changes through becoming clearer about what they want from them and justifying those desires to the others involved. That is the sort of process *within* relationships that corresponds to what Habermas and Rawls postulate as a process of reform from without. In relationships characterized by reciprocity this sort of process is achievable. It is the same process as leads to constant modifications in people's loves, friendships and fraternal bonds. No grandiose changes need be envisaged, but major changes may nonetheless occur as a result.

Where, however, relationships are skewed by disparities of power there may be nothing that can be done to change them from within. Then it is only through forming other relationships in which people have a common purpose and an equal stake that the disempowered can challenge the empowered. The extreme case of this is social revolution. For social revolution cannot come about without the formation of communal groups. However uniform its grievances, 'a class is not in itself a community', as the sociologist Max Weber saw (cp. Bottomore, p. 97). What may seem to sweep away social relationships, then, itself depends upon utilizing their most basic forms. To lose these is unthinkable. But to overlook them is all too easy.

Further reading

An interesting discussion of relationships and arguments for loosening them is Brenda Almond's 'Human Bonds'. Plato's *Republic*, books 5–7, describes his ideal state: the classic contemporary rejection of similar projects is Karl Popper's *The Open Society and its Enemies*. To what extent is it *possible* to design the sort of society in which we would wish to live, rather than simply patching up defects in the present one?

Peter Winch's 'Understanding a Primitive Society' is a seminal text on the problems of comparing different social practices. How *might* we debate the merits of monogamy with an Arab or a Tibetan? Can we think of any of our own social values as *thoroughly* undesirable?

Bibliography

Albee, Edward, *Who's Afraid of Virginia Woolf?*, London, Cape, 1964.

Almond, Brenda, 'Human Bonds', *Journal of Applied Philosophy*, 5, 1988.

Ardrey, Robert, *The Territorial Imperative*, London, Collins, 1967.

Aristotle, (E), *Nicomachean Ethics*, trans. J. A. K. Thomson, Harmondsworth, Penguin, 1953.

Aristotle, (P), *Politics*, trans. T. A. Sinclair, Harmondsworth, Penguin, 1962.

Atkinson, Ti Grace, 'Radical Feminism' in A. M. Jagger and P. S. Rothenberg, (eds), *Feminist Frameworks*, New York, McGraw-Hill, 1984.

Austen, Jane, *Sense and Sensibility* (1811) (many editions).

Barnard, F. M., 'Will and Political Rationality in Rousseau' in J. Lively and A. Reese (eds), *Modern Political Theory from Hobbes to Marx: Key Debates*, London, Routledge, 1989.

Becker, Lawrence C., *Reciprocity*, London, Routledge, 1986.

Benn, S. I. and Gauss G. F. (eds), *Public and Private in Social Life*, London, Croom Helm, 1983.

Benn, S. I., *A Theory of Freedom*, Cambridge, Cambridge University Press, 1988.

Bentham, Jeremy, *Principles of Morals and Legislation* (1789), reprinted in *The Utilitarians*, New York, Doubleday, 1961.

Beran, Harry, *The Consent Theory of Political Obligation*, London, Croom Helm, 1987.

Berger, Peter L., *Invitation to Sociology*, Harmondsworth, Penguin, 1963.

Blum, L., *Friendship, Altruism and Morality*, London, Routledge, 1980.

Bottomore, Thomas, *Political Sociology*, London, Hutchinson, 1979.

Bowen, Elizabeth, (D), *The Death of the Heart*, London, Cape, 1949.

Bowen, Elizabeth, (HD), *The Heat of the Day*, London, Cape and Reprint Society, 1950.

Bowen, Elizabeth, (H), *The Hotel*, Harmondsworth, Penguin, 1984.

Brontë, Charlotte, *Jane Eyre* (1847) (many editions).

Brown, Roger, *Analysing Love*, Cambridge, Cambridge University Press, 1981.

Butler, (Bishop) Joseph, *Sermons* (1726) (many editions).

Cohen (later Almond), Brenda, 'Positive Values', *Aristotelian Society Suppl. Vol. LVII*, 1983.

Cole, G. D. H. and Postgate, Raymond, *The Common People 1746–1938*, London, Methuen, 1938.

Collier, Andrew, (S), 'Scientific Socialism and the Question of Socialist Values' in J. Mepham and D. H. Ruben (eds), *Issues in Marxist Philosophy*, vol. IV, Brighton, Harvester, 1979.

Collier, Andrew, (P), 'Positive Values', *Aristotelian Society Suppl. Vol. LVII*, 1983.

Collins, Randall, *Conflict Sociology*, New York, Academic Press, 1975.

Conrad, Joseph, 'An Anarchist', in *A Set of Six* (1908) (many editions).

Coward, Rosalind, *Female Desire*, London, Paladin, 1984.

Dancy, Jonathan, *An Introduction to Contemporary Epistemology*, Oxford, Basil Blackwell, 1985.

de Beauvoir, Simone, *The Second Sex*, Harmondsworth, Penguin, 1972.

Descartes, René, *Meditations* (1641) (many editions).

Dickens, Charles, *Dombey and Son* (1847) (many editions).

Dilman, Ilham, *Freud and Human Nature*, Oxford, Basil Blackwell, 1983.

Dilman, Ilham, *Love and Human Separateness*, Oxford, Basil Blackwell, 1987.

Duck, Steve, *Human Relationships*, London, Sage, 1986.

Durkheim, Emile, *The Rules of Sociological Method*, Chicago, Chicago University Press, 1950.

Eibl-Eibesfeldt, Irenaus, *Love and Hate*, trans. G. Strachan, London, Methuen, 1971.

Engels, Friedrich, *The Origins of the Family, Private Property and the State*, Moscow, Foreign Languages Publishing House, 1943.

Farb, Peter, *Man's Rise to Civilisation*, London, Paladin, 1971.

Fisher, Mark, 'Reason, Emotion and Love', *Inquiry* 20, 1977.

Foucault, Michel, *The History of Sexuality*, Harmondsworth, Penguin, 1981.

Freud, Sigmund, *Complete Psychological Works*, vol. VII, including 'Three Essays on Sexuality', trans. J. Strachan, London, Hogarth Press, 1953.

Freud, Sigmund, *Complete Psychological Works*, vol. XVIII, including 'Group Psychology', trans. J. Strachan, London, Hogarth Press, 1953.

Fried, Charles, *An Anatomy of Values*, Cambridge, Mass., Harvard University Press, 1970.

Gadamer, Hans Georg, *Truth and Method*, trans. and ed. G. Barden and J. Cumming, London, Sheed and Ward, 1975.

Garnett, David, (L), *Lady into Fox*, London, Chatto and Windus, 1928.

Garnett, David, (S), *A Shot in the Dark*, Harmondsworth, Penguin, 1962.

Gaskell, Mrs Elizabeth, *Sylvia's Lovers* (1863) (many editions).

Giddens, Anthony, *The Nation-State and Violence*, Cambridge, Polity Press, 1985.

Goethe, J. W. von, *Poetry and Truth*, vol. 1, trans. M. S. Smith, London, Bell, 1913.

Gorer, Geoffrey, *The Life and Ideas of the Marquis de Sade*, London, Panther, 1964.

Gould, Carol, *Rethinking Democracy*, Cambridge, Cambridge University Press, 1988.

Graham, Gordon, *Contemporary Social Philosophy*, Oxford, Basil Blackwell, 1988.

Graham, Keith, (BD), *The Battle of Democracy*, Brighton, Wheatsheaf, 1986.

Grant, Vernon W., *Falling in Love*, New York, Springer, 1976.

Greene, Graham, *The Heart of the Matter*, London, Heinemann, 1948.

Gregory, Paul, 'Against Couples', *Journal of Applied Philosophy*, 2, 1985.

Habermas, Jurgen, (LC), *Legitimation Crisis*, London, Heinemann, 1976.

Habermas, Jurgen, (R), 'A Review of Gadamer's *Truth and Method*', in F. R. Dallmayr and T. A. McCarthy (eds), *Understanding Social Inquiry*, Notre Dame, Indiana University Press, 1977.

Halsey, A. H., *Change in British Society*, Oxford: Oxford University Press, 1987.

Heidegger, Martin, *Being and Time*, trans. J. McQuarrie, London, SCM Press, 1962.

Hobbes, Thomas, *Leviathan* (1651) (many editions).

Holtby, Winifred, *South Riding*, London, Collins, 1936.

Howells, Christine, *Sartre: The necessity of freedom*, Cambridge, Cambridge University Press, 1988.

Hume, David, (E), *Essays, Moral and Political* (1741–2) (many editions).

Hume, David, (T), *Treatise of Human Nature* (1739–40) (many editions).

James, Henry, *The American* (1877) (many editions).

Kant, Immanuel, *The Moral Law*, [Kant's 'Groundwork of the Metaphysic of Morals'], trans. H. J. Paton, London, Hutchinson, 1961.

Kaufmann, Walter, *Nietzsche*, Princeton, Princeton University Press, 1968.

Keynes, J. M., *Two Memoirs*, London, Rupert Hart-Davies, 1949.

Kierkegaard, Søren, (E), *Either/Or, A Kiekegaard Anthology*, ed. Robert Bretall, Princeton, Princeton University Press, 1946.

Kierkegaard, Søren, (W), *Works of Love, A Kierkegaard Anthology*, ed. Robert Bretall, Princeton, Princeton University Press, 1946.

Kroptkin, (Prince) Peter, *Mutual Aid*, Harmondsworth, Penguin, 1939.

Lacan, J., *The Four Fundamental Concepts of Psychoanalysis*, Harmondsworth, Penguin, 1979.

La Rochefoucauld, *Maxims*, trans. L. W. Tancock, Harmondsworth, Penguin, 1959.

Lawrence, D. H., (AR), *Aaron's Rod*, London, Heinemann, 1935.

Lawrence, D. H., (L), *The Letters of D. H. Lawrence*, ed. A. Huxley, London, Heinemann, 1932.

Lienhardt, Godfrey, *Social Anthropology*, London, Oxford University Press, 1966.

Locke, John, 'Second Treatise on Civil Government' (1690) (reprinted in *Social Contract*, London, Oxford University Press, 1947).

Lorenz, Konrad, *On Aggression*, London, Methuen, 1966.

Lukes, Steven (ed.), *Power*, Oxford, Basil Blackwell, 1986.

Mabbott, J. D., *The State and the Citizen*, London, Hutchinson, 1947.

McCoubrey, H., *The Development of Naturalist Legal Theory*, London, Croom Helm, 1987.

Mair, Lucy, (PG), *Primitive Government*, Harmondsworth, Penguin, 1962.

Mair, Lucy, (I), *An Introduction to Social Anthropology*, Oxford, Oxford University Press, 1965.

Maugham, Somerset, *Of Human Bondage*, London, Heinemann, (collected edition) 1937.

Maurois, André, *Seven Faces of Love*, London, John Lane, 1948.

Merleau-Ponty, Maurice, *Phenomenology of Perception*, trans. Colin Smith, London, Routledge, 1962.

Milne, A. J. M., *Human Rights and Human Diversity*, London, Macmillan, 1986.

Mitchell, Juliet, *Woman's Estate*, Harmondsworth, Penguin, 1971.

Moore, G. E., *Principia Ethica*, Cambridge, Cambridge University Press, 1954.

Morrison, Toni, *The Bluest Eye*, London, Triad Grafton, 1981.

Munch, Richard, *Understanding Modernity*, London, Routledge, 1988.

Murdoch, Iris, *Sartre: romantic rationalist*, London, Fontana, 1967.

Nagel, Thomas, *Mortal Questions*, Cambridge, Cambridge University Press, 1979.

Nietzsche, Friedrich, (GS), *The Gay Science*, trans. W. Kaufmann, New York, Random House, 1974.

Nietzsche, Friedrich, (G), *On the Genealogy of Morals and Ecce Homo*, trans. W. Kaufmann, New York, Random House, 1969.

Nietzsche, Friedrich, (Z), *Thus Spake Zarathustra*, trans. R. J. Hollingdale, Harmondsworth, Penguin, 1969.

Peters, R. S., (C), *The Concept of Motivation*, London, Routledge, 1958.

Peters, R. S., (E), *Ethics and Education*, London, Allen and Unwin, 1966.

Phillips, Robert, *Just and Unjust Wars*, New York, Basic, 1973.

Plato, (P), *Phaedrus* (many editions; references are given to the marginal section numbers).

Plato, (R), *Republic*, trans. H. D. P. Lee, Harmondsworth, Penguin, 1955.

Plato, (S), *Symposium*, trans. B. Jowett, Oxford, Oxford University Press, 1875.

Popper, Karl, *The Open Society and its Enemies*, London, Routledge, 1945.

Price, A. W., *Love and Friendship in Plato and Aristotle*, Oxford, Oxford University Press, 1989.

Putnam, Hilary, *Reason, Truth and History*, Cambridge, Cambridge University Press, 1981.

Raphael, D. D., *Problems of Political Philosophy*, London, Macmillan, 1976.

Rawls, John, (J), *A Theory of Justice*, Oxford, Oxford University Press, 1973.

Rawls, John, (R), 'Two Concepts of Rules', *Philosophical Review*, 64, 1955.

Reiman, Jeffrey, 'Privacy, Intimacy and Personhood', *Philosophy and Public Affairs*, 6, 1976–7.

Rosenberg, Alexander, *Philosophy of Social Science*, Oxford, Oxford University Press, 1988.

Rousseau, Jean-Jacques, *The Social Contract* (reprinted in *Social Contract*, London, Oxford University Press), 1947.

Rubin, Z., *Liking and Loving*, New York, Holt, Rinehart and Winston, 1973.

Ruskin, John, *Sesame and Lilies* (1865) (many editions).

Sabine, George H., *A History of Political Theory*, London, Harrap, 1963.

Santas, G., *Plato and Freud: Two Theories of Love*, Oxford, Basil Blackwell, 1988.

Sartre, John Paul, (BN) *Being and Nothingness*, trans. H. E. Barnes, London, Methuen, 1969.

Sartre, John Paul, *Critique of Dialectical Reason*, trans. A. Sheridan-Smith, London, Verso, 1976.

Schopenhauer, Alfred, *The World as Will and Representative*, vol. II, trans. E. F. J. Payne, New York, Dover, 1958.

Scruton, Roger, *Sexual Desire*, London, Weidenfeld and Nicholson, 1986.

Selsam, H. and Martel, H., *Reader in Marxist Philosophy*, New York, International Publishers, 1963.

Shaftesbury, Anthony Ashley Cooper, Earl of, *An Inquiry Concerning Virtue* (1699), reprinted in L. A. Selby-Biggs (ed.), *British Moralists*, Indianapolis, Bobbs Merrill, 1964.

Sidgwick, Henry, *Methods of Ethics*, London, Macmillan, 1907.

Smith, P. and Jones, O. R., *The Philosophy of Mind*, Cambridge, Cambridge University Press, 1986.

Spencer, Herbert, *The Man versus the State*, London, Watts, 1940.

Stafford, J. M., 'Love and Lust Revisited', *Journal of Applied Philosophy*, 1988.

Stephen, Sir James Fitzjames, *Liberty, Equality, Fraternity*, London, Smith, Elder, 1873.

Strawson, P. F., 'Social Morality and the Individual Ideal', *Philosophy*, 1961.

Taylor, R. L., 'Sexual Experiences', *Proceedings of the Aristotelian Society*, 1967.

Toennies, Ferdinand, *On Sociology: Pure, Applied and Empirical*, Chicago, Chicago University Press, 1971.

Tolstoy, Leo, (ET) *Essays from Tula*, London, Sheppard Press, 1948.

Tolstoy, Leo, (K) *The Kreutzer Sonata*, trans. A. Maude, Oxford, Oxford University Press, 1950.

Turnbull, Colin, *The Mountain People*, London, Pan, 1974.

Vernon, Grant W., *Falling in Love*, New York, Springer, 1976.

Walster, E. and G. W., *A New Look at Love*, Reading, Mass., Addison Wesley, 1978.

Wells, H. G., *A Short History of the World*, London, Waterlow, 1933.

Wilson, E. O., *On Human Nature*, Cambridge, Mass., Harvard University Press, 1978.

Winch, Peter, 'Understanding a Primitive Society', in his *Ethics and Action*, London, Routledge, 1972.

Wisdom, John, *Other Minds*, Oxford, Basil Blackwell, 1952.

Woolf, Virginia, *To the Lighthouse* (1927) reprinted London, Granada, 1977.

Wordsworth, William, *The Prelude* (1850) (many editions).

Wright, Derek, *The Psychology of Moral Behaviour*, Harmondsworth, Penguin, 1971.

Index